COMMUNION AND LIBERATION

COMMUNION AND LIBERATION

A Movement in the Church

Edited by Davide Rondoni

Translated by Patrick Stevenson
and Susan Scott

Published for
Cooperativa Editoriale Nuovo Mondo
by
McGill-Queen's University Press
Montreal & Kingston · London · Ithaca

© McGill-Queen's University Press 2000
ISBN 978-0-7735-2031-8 (paper)
ISBN 978-0-7735-6829-7 (ePDF)

Legal deposit first quarter 2000
Bibliothèque nationale du Québec
Reprinted 2013

Printed in Canada on acid-free paper that is 100%
ancient forest free (100% post-consumer recycled),
processed chlorine free

McGill-Queen's University Press acknowledges
the financial support of the Government of Canada
through the Canada Book Fund for its activities.
We also acknowledge the support of the Canada
Council for the Arts for our publishing program.

This book was first published in 1998 by
Cooperativa Editoriale Nuovo Mondo under
the title *Comunione e liberazione:
Un movimento nella Chiesa.*

Canadian Cataloguing in Publication Data

Main entry under title:
Communion and liberation: a movement in the church
Translation of: Comunione e liberazione: un movi-
mento nella chiesa, published: Milan: Nuovo Mondo,
c1998.
Includes bibliographical references.
ISBN 978-0-7735-2031-8 (paper)
ISBN 978-0-7735-6829-7 (ePDF)
1. Comunione e liberazione.
I. Rondoni, Davide, 1964–
BX814.C663C6413 1999   267'.182   C99-901325-4

This book was typeset by Typo Litho
Composition Inc. in 10/13 Palatino.

CONTENTS

INTRODUCTORY NOTE

This booklet was prepared to provide useful information about the movement called "Communion and Liberation" (CL). It is obvious that the characteristics of such a phenomenon are, by their very nature, impossible to summarize and lay out in a schematic way. We have tried, therefore, to offer a series of basic readings which start by explaining what a movement within the Catholic Church is and why CL is defined as being such a movement. Next, the essential elements of the educational proposal envisioned by Father Giussani are described. A brief biographical profile of the founder of CL is given, followed by historical notes about the movement, from its inception in 1954 to today. In reviewing its history, we highlight some of the most important characteristics of the method and the theoretical formulation that derive from experience of the movement. These characteristics are further described and more fully explained in the chapter on life in CL. Finally, brief outlines of some forms of life in community that have arisen from the experience of CL are offered. An ample appendix of documents pertaining to the movement brings the book to its close.

A MOVEMENT IN THE CHURCH

RECOGNIZING CHRIST[*]

This morning's meditation ended with Kafka's strikingly effective image that: "There is a point of arrival but no way."[1] It is undeniable that there is an "unknown" (the geographers of ancient times traced the outline of what amounts to an analogue of this unknown with the famous expression *terra incognita* that marked the edge of their great sheet – along the margins of the sheet they wrote *terra incognita*, "unknown land"). At the edge of reality that the eye embraces, the heart feels, and the mind imagines, there is an unknown. Everyone feels it. Everyone has always felt it. Throughout the ages men have felt it so strongly that they have also imagined it. In every age men have sought, through their ponderings or fantasies, to imagine, to fix the face of this unknown. In his *Germania*, Tacitus described the religious feeling that distinguished the ancient Teutons thus: "*Secretum illud quod sola reverentia vident, hoc deum appellant*" (that mysterious thing which they intuited with fear and trembling, this they called God, this they call God).[2] All men of all ages, however they have imagined it,

* Notes of a meditation by Monsignor Luigi Giussani for CL university students who gathered for spiritual exercises; now "Riconoscere Cristo" in L. Giussani, *Il tempo e il tempio* (Milan: 1995), pp. 39–50.

hoc deum appellant, call this "unknown" God, before whom the indifferent gazes of most, but the impassioned of many, pass by. Undoubtedly among the impassioned ones were the three hundred people who walked in procession with Cardinal Martini from the church of San Carlo to Milan Cathedral. Three hundred representatives of different religions! And what can we call, as a common denominator, that which they intended to express and honour by their participation in the Cardinal of Milan's great initiative? A *secretum illud*, something mysterious, an unknown land, something unknowable – unknowable!

I would like to recall now a comparison which can be found in the second volume of the School of Community[3] series (those who have already read it will recognize it). Imagine the human world, human history, as an immense plain, and on this immense plain there is an immense crowd of companies, construction companies, particularly experienced in the making of roads and bridges. Each one in its corner, from its corner, tries to launch a bridge from the point where they are, the ephemeral moment in which they are living, right up to the sky studded with stars, echoing Victor Hugo's image in his beautiful poem entitled *"Le Pont"* ("The Bridge") from *Les Contemplations*.[4] He imagines someone, a man, sitting on a beach one starry night, staring at the largest star, apparently the one closest to him, and thinking of the thousands and thousands of arches that would have to be built to construct this bridge, a bridge never fully defined, never completely usable. Imagine, then, this immense plain, crowded with attempts by groups large and small, or even individuals, as in Hugo's image, each one carrying out his imagined, fantastic design. Suddenly a powerful voice is heard in the immense plain, saying, "Stop! All of you stop!" And all the workers, engineers, architects stop working and look toward where the voice is coming from: it is a man, who continues, raising his arm: "You are great men, your efforts are noble, but your attempt, albeit great and noble, is a sad one. This is why so many give up and stop thinking about it and become indifferent. It is great but sad, because it will never end, it will never reach its goal. You are not able to do it because you are impotent in front of this aim. There is an insurmountable disproportion between you and the farthest star in the sky, between you and God. You cannot imagine the Mystery. Now leave your hard thankless work and follow me: I will build this bridge for you, rather, *I am* this bridge! Because *I am the way,* the truth, the life!"[5]

The real intellectual value of such things cannot be understood if we do not make ourselves one with them, if we do not try to merge with them with our hearts. Imagine that, on the sand dunes near the sea, you see a small group of people from the nearby village listening to someone speaking in the middle of the group; and you pass by to go to the beach you are heading for; you pass close by and as you pass you look curiously and you hear the man in the middle say: "I am the way, the truth, the life! I am the way, the

truth …" The way which cannot be known, of which
Kafka spoke: "I am the way, the truth, the life." Imagine, make an effort of the imagination, of fantasy, what
would you do, what would you say? No matter how
skeptical you are, you cannot but prick up your ears,
attracted by something coming from that direction,
and, at the very least, you look very curiously at that
man who is either mad or is telling the truth – *tertium
not datur*: either he is mad or he is true. As a matter of
fact, he is so true that there has been only one man,
only one, who has said this, one in the whole history
of the world – of the world! A man in the midst of a
small group of people, often in the midst of a small
group but often amidst a big crowd, too.

So everyone in the plain stops working to listen
carefully to this voice, and he keeps repeating the
same words. Who were the first to be annoyed by all
this? The engineers, architects, and owners of the construction companies, who said, practically immediately: "Come on, men, back to work! Workers, back to
your jobs! That man's just a braggart!" He was a radical alternative, *tranchant*, to their project, to their creativity, their earnings, their power, their name, to
themselves. He was the alternative to themselves. After the engineers, architects, and bosses turn back, so,
too, do the workers, who more reluctantly dragged
their eyes away from the man, beginning to laugh a
bit, talking about him for awhile, making fun of him
or saying, "Who knows, who knows who he is. Could
he be mad?" But some of them did not turn away.

Some heard a tone they had never heard before, and they did not answer the engineer, architect, or building contractor who said to them: "Come on, hurry up, what are you doing here, what are you still looking at over there?" Instead, they kept looking at the man. And he came forward. Or rather, they went toward him. Out of 120 million people, there were twelve who did this. But it happened: *this is a historical fact*.

What Kafka says ("there is no way") is not historically true. Paradoxically, one could say that it is true theoretically but it is not true historically. The mystery cannot be known! This is true theoretically. But if the mystery knocks on your door ... "If anyone hears my voice and opens the door, I will enter his house and dine with him,"[6] are words you can read in the Bible, the word of God in the Bible. But it really happened.

The first chapter of the Gospel of St John, which is the first page in literature to speak of it, along with the general announcement "The Word was made flesh" – that of which all reality is made was made man – contains the memories of those who followed him immediately, who resisted the urgency imposed on them by the engineers and architects. On a piece of paper, one of them noted his first impressions and what the first moment was like when it happened. Indeed the first chapter of John contains a series of notes which are precisely that, notes from memory. One of the two men, in his old age, read in his memory the notes that remained there. Because memory has its own law. The law of memory is not a continuity without gaps, as is, for example, a fantastic creation from imagination; memory literally "takes notes," as we do now: a note, a line, a point, and this point covers lots of things, so that the second phrase starts out from the many things supposed by the first point. Things are supposed more than said, some are only said as points of reference. So that I at my seventy years of age reread them for the thousandth time, without any trace of tiredness. I challenge you to imagine anything that is more serious, more weighty, in the sense of *pondus*, greater, more charged with challenge for human existence in its apparent fragility, more pregnant with consequences in history, than this fact which happened.

"The next day John was there again with two of his disciples, and as he watched Jesus walk by he said ..." Imagine the scene, then. After 150 years of waiting, the Hebrew people, who throughout their whole history, for two thousand years, had always had some prophet, someone recognized by all as a prophet, after 150 years they finally had a prophet again: he was called John the Baptist. Other writings from antiquity speak of him, so he is historically documented. Everyone – rich and poor, publicans and Pharisees, friends and foes – went to hear him and to see how he lived, beyond the Jordan, in the desert, feeding on locusts and wild herbs. He always had a group of people around him. Among these people that day were also two who were there for the first time and had come, we would say, from the country – really they came from the lake, which was quite far away and outside the area of the developed cities. They were there like two villagers who have come to the city for the first time, a bit lost, and they looked at everything around them wide-eyed, especially at him. They were there with their mouths open and their eyes popping out, looking at him, listening to him, so attentively.

Suddenly someone in the group, a young man, sets out, taking the path along the river heading north. And John the Baptist, fixing his gaze on him, shouts: "Behold the Lamb of God, behold the one who takes away the sins of the world!" But the people did not move; they were used to hearing the prophet come out every once in a while with strange, incomprehensible, unconnected phrases, out of context; so most of them took no notice. The two who were there for the first time and were hanging on his every word and watching his eyes, looking wherever he looked, saw that John was staring at the man who was leaving, and they set off at his heels. They followed him at a distance, timid and ashamed, but strangely, profoundly, obscurely curious, intrigued. "The two disciples heard what he said and followed Jesus. Jesus turned and saw them following him and said to them, 'What are you looking for?' They said to him, 'Rabbi, where are you staying?' He said to them, 'Come, and you will see.'" This is the formula, *the* Christian formula. This is the Christian method: "Come and see." "So they went and saw where he was staying, and they stayed with him that day. It was about four in the afternoon." It does not specify when they left, when they followed him; the whole passage and the following one are made up of notes, as I said before; the sentences end at a point which takes for granted that many things are already known. For example: "It was about four in the afternoon;" does this mean when they left, or when they went there, who knows? In any case, it was four in the afternoon. One of the two who had heard the words of John the Baptist and followed him was named Andrew; he was Simon Peter's brother. The first person he met was his brother Simon coming back from the beach – he was coming back from fishing or from mending his fishing nets – and he said to him: "We have found the Messiah." He doesn't narrate anything, doesn't say what anybody said, doesn't furnish proof – it is well-known, it is clear, these are notes about things that everybody knows! Very few pages can be read that are so realistically true to life, so simply true to life, where not one word has been added to pure reminiscence.

How could he say: "We have found the Messiah"? Jesus, in talking to them, would have used this word, which was part of their vocabulary; because saying that this man was the Messiah, "just like that" so convincedly, would have been impossible. But it is evident that staying there listening to this man for hours and hours, seeing him, watching him speak – who could speak like that? Who had ever talked like that? Who had said those things? They were unheard of! No one had ever seen anyone like that! – slowly within their minds the idea was growing: "If I don't believe this man I'll never believe anybody, not even my own eyes." Not that they said it, not that they thought it, they felt rather than thought it. So that man must have said, among other things, that he was the one who was to come, the Messiah who was to come. But the exceptionality of the proclamation made it so obvious that they came away with that statement as though it were something simple – it was simple! – as though it were something easy to understand.

"He brought Simon to Jesus, who looked at him and said, 'You are Simon son of John; you shall be called Cephas' (that is, Peter, 'the Rock')." It was a Jewish custom to give someone a new name to indicate their character or commemorate something that happened. So, imagine Simon who goes with his brother, full of curiosity and some fear, and he stares at the man his brother has brought him to see. That man is also staring at him while he is still far away. Think of how he is staring at him, to the point that he has understood his character to the very marrow of his bones: "You will be called Rock." Think of how someone feels when looked at like that by someone new, a complete stranger, grasped to the depths of his being. "The next day Jesus decided to leave for Galilee ..." The rest you can read for yourselves. It is half a page like this, made up of brief notes and points in which it is taken for granted that everyone knew everything that had happened, that it was evident to all.

"There is a point of arrival, but no way." No! A man who said: "I am the way" is *a historical fact which hap-*

pened, first described in this half page that I have
started to read. And every one of us knows that it happened. Nothing in the world ever happened that was
as unthinkable and exceptional as the man of whom
we are speaking: Jesus of Nazareth.

But those two, the first two, John and Andrew –
Andrew was most probably married with children –
how was it that they were won over so quickly and
recognized him (there is no other word that can be
used, than recognize)? I would say that if this fact happened, recognizing that man, who that man was, not
who he was in detail, in the depths of his being, but
recognizing that this man was something exceptional,
out of the ordinary – he was absolutely out of the ordinary – irreducible by any form of analysis, recognizing
this must have been easy. If God became man and
came among us, if he came now, if he slipped into our
crowd and were here now among us, recognizing him,
I say *a priori*, should be *easy*: easy to recognize him as
divine. Why is it easy to recognize him? Because of an
exceptionality, an exceptionality beyond compare. I
have in front of me an exceptionality, an exceptional
man, beyond compare. What does exceptional mean?
What can it mean? Why does the exceptional strike
you? Why do you feel something "exceptional" to be
exceptional? Because it *corresponds* to the expectations
of your heart, no matter how confused and nebulous
they might be. It corresponds unexpectedly – unexpectedly! – to the needs of your mind or your heart, to
the irresistible, undeniable demands of your heart in a

way you could never have imagined or predicted, because there is no one like this man. The exceptional is, paradoxically, the appearance of what is most natural for us. What is natural for me? That what I want happens. More natural than this! That what I most want most happens: this is natural. To come across something totally, profoundly natural, because it corresponds to the demands of the heart that nature gave us, is something absolutely exceptional. It is like a strange contradiction: what happens is never exceptional, truly exceptional, because it does not succeed in responding adequately to the heart's demands. We approach exceptionality when something makes the heart beat for a correspondence that we think is valuable and that the events of tomorrow will retract and next year annul.

It is the exceptionality with which the figure of Christ appears that makes it easy to recognize him. We must imagine ourselves, as I said before, we must submerge ourselves in these events. If we try to judge them, if we want to judge them – I don't say understand them, but judge them substantially, as true or false – it is the sincerity of your identification with them that makes the true true and not false, and does not make your heart doubt the truth. It is easy to recognize it as a divine ontology because it is exceptional: it corresponds to the heart, and you *stay with it* and never want to leave – which is the sign of a correspondence with the heart. One would never leave, and would follow him for one's whole life. And in fact they followed him for the three more years that he lived.

But imagine those two who stay there listening to him for hours and then they have to go home. He says goodbye to them and they go their way silently, silent because full of the impression they have received of the felt mystery, about which they had had a feeling beforehand and then they had actually felt. And then they separate. Each of the two goes to his own house. They don't say goodbye, not because they don't say goodbye but because they bid each other farewell without saying goodbye, because they are both full of the same thing, the two of them are one, so full are they of the same thing. And Andrew goes into his house and puts his cloak down, and his wife says: "Andrew, what's wrong with you? You're different, what happened?" Imagine that he burst into tears in her arms, and that she, upset by all this, continued to ask him: "But what's wrong?" And he, holding his wife, who had never felt herself held that way before, he was a different person. He was a different person! He was the same, but he was different. If anyone had asked him; "Who are you?" he would have said; "I understand that I have become someone else ... after hearing that person, that man, I have become another person." My friends, without going too much into it, this happened.

Not only is it easy to recognize him, it was easy to recognize him in his exceptionality – because "if I don't believe this man then I don't even believe my own eyes any more"[7] – but it was easy to understand

what type of morality, that is, what type of relationship, was born with him, because morality is the relationship with reality insofar as it is created from the
mystery that made it; it is the proper, orderly relationship with reality. It was easy, for them it was easy to
understand how easy the relationship with him was,
how easy it was to follow him, to be consistent with
what he was, to be consistent with his presence – consistent with his presence –.

There is another page from St John's writings that
says these things in a really wonderful way: it is in the
last chapter of his Gospel, the twenty-first. That morning the boat was coming to shore and they hadn't
caught any fish. A few hundred meters from the water's edge they realized there was a man standing
there – he had lit a fire, they could see it from one hundred meters away – who started talking to them in a
way that I won't go into right now. John was the first
to say, "It is the Lord!," and Saint Peter threw himself
into the water and in four strokes reached the shore;
and it is the Lord. In the meantime the others arrive,
and no one talks. They gather around in a circle, and
no one speaks, everyone is quiet, because everyone
knows that it is the risen Lord: he had already died
and had already shown himself to them after he had
risen. He had grilled some fish for them. Everyone sits
and eats. In the almost total silence that weighes on
the beach, Jesus, lying down, looks at the man next to
him, who was Simon Peter; he stares at him, and Peter
felt, we can imagine how he felt, the weight of that

gaze, because he remembered his betrayal of a few weeks earlier, and of everything that he had done – he had even been called Satan by Christ: "Get behind me, Satan, you are a stumbling block for me, for the destiny of my life"[8] – he remembered all his faults, because when you make a terrible mistake in your life, you remember all the other things you have done, even those that are not so terrible. Peter felt as if he was crushed by the weight of his incapacity, his inability to be a man. And that man next to him opened his mouth and said: "Simon [imagine how Simon must have been trembling], do you love me?" But, if you try to put yourselves in this situation, you will tremble now thinking about it, just thinking about it, thinking about this scene that was so dramatic: dramatic because it is so descriptive of what is human, showing what is human, exalting what is human, because drama is what exalts the human element; only tragedy annihilates it. Nihilism leads to tragedy; the encounter with Christ brings drama into your life, because drama is the relationship lived between an I and a you. Then, like a sigh, like a sigh Peter answers. His response is barely hinted, like a sigh. He doesn't dare, but … "I don't know how, yes, Lord, I love you; I don't know how, but that's how it is" (as in the video some of us saw a few weeks ago).[9] "Yes, Lord. I don't know how, I can't tell you how, but …"

In short, it was very easy to maintain, to live, the relationship with that man, all one had to do was adhere to the sympathy that he aroused, a *profound sympathy*, similar to that dizzying, visceral relationship between a baby and its mother, which is sympathy in the intense meaning of the word. It was enough to adhere to the sympathy that he aroused. Because, after everything that Peter had done to him, the betrayal and all, he heard him say: "Simon, do you love me?" Three times. And the third time he suspected, maybe, that there was some doubt underlying the question, and he answered more completely: "Lord, you know everything, you know that I love you. My human sympathy is for you; my human sympathy is for you, Jesus of Nazareth."

Luigi Giussani

COMMUNION AND LIBERATION: A MOVEMENT

1.1. A REALITY IN THE CHURCH

Communion and Liberation is an ecclesiastical movement founded by Msgr. Luigi Giussani; its earliest manifestations date to 1954. Having arisen in Milan and spread rapidly throughout Italy, it is now present in some seventy countries all over the world.

CL is a reality among those movements recognized authoritatively by the Church as "co-essential"[10] to her own nature, in that it is "a certain way in which the relationship between God and humans, which takes the name of Christ, becomes a present reality."[11] The Church, in fact, recognizes that "the charism of the Spirit always creates affinities," and that "the Spirit, in order to pursue with contemporary man that dialogue initiated by God in Christ and continuing through all of Christian history, has brought forth numerous movements within the Church. These are a sign of the many different ways in which the one Church is realized."[12]

CL defines itself as a movement because it does not take the form of a new organization or structure (there are no membership cards) nor is it a special insistence on some particular aspect or practice of the life of the faith. Instead, it is a call to live in the present the Christian experience as defined by tradition. The aim of life in CL is to propose the presence of Christ as the only true response to the deepest needs of human life in every moment of history. In the person who encounters and adheres to the presence of Christ there is generated a *movement* of conversion and witness, which tends to leave its mark on the environment in which he or she lives (family, work, school, neighborhood, society, etc.).

Born in the schools as a proposal to young people, today CL extends its call to everyone, irrespective of age, occupation, or social position.

1.2. WHAT IS A CHARISM?

Recently, answering those who asked him what is meant by "charism" and what is the specific nature of the charism that gave birth to Communion and Liberation, Msgr Giussani responded:

Synthetically, a charism can be defined as a gift of the Spirit, given to a person in a specific historical context, so that this person can initiate an experience of faith that might in some way be useful to the life of the Church. I emphasize the existential nature of charism: it makes the Christian message handed down by the apostolic tradition more convincing, more persuasive, more "approachable" ... This emphasis makes the proposal of faith existential. I often say that a charism is an ultimate terminal of the Incarnation: that is, it is a particular way in which the Fact of Jesus Christ Man and God reaches me and, through me, can reach others. This comes about through a human encounter ... The reality generated by a charismatic gift is the outermost and contingent point in which the event of Christ becomes present. And yet, in its precariousness, it is the most important point for a person's life, because through that ephemeral terminal he is reached by the great Presence where he lives. How did Christ communicate himself two thousand years ago? Through a concrete event. John and Andrew were struck by his presence on the banks of the Jordan and ... they went to see where he lived. Our movement is nothing more than one of the many manifestations of this method.

1.3. THE CHARISM OF CL

Msgr. Giussani continues:

The charism of Communion and Liberation is not determined by any specifically defined "sector." I would say rather that the original nature of our movement lies in the insistence on the method of how the Christian experience can be lived. In this sense, if I had to indicate its essence, I would say it is signaled by two factors. First, the announcement that God became man, the companion in history on our human path. Second, the affirmation that Jesus of Nazareth is present in a sign of harmony, of communion, of community, of unity: the Church, His mysterious body. From these two elements arises that missionary passion that He be known and recognized as Lord of time and of history ... From the first hour of class at the Berchet High

School in Milan I tried to show the students what moved me: not the wish to convince them that I was right but the desire to show them the reasonableness of faith: that is, that their free adhesion to the Christian proclamation was demanded by their discovery of the correspondence of what I was saying with the needs of their hearts, as implied by the definition of reasonableness. Only this dynamic of recognition makes whoever adheres to our movement creative and a protagonist and not simply one who repeats formulas and things they have heard. For this reason, it seems to me, a charism generates a social phenomenon not as something planned but as a movement of persons who have been changed by an encounter; who tentatively make the world, the environment, and the circumstances that they encounter more human. The memory of Christ when it is lived tends inevitably to generate a presence in society, above and beyond any planned result.[13]

1.4. FUNDAMENTAL PEDAGOGICAL LINES

CL has always been defined as an ecclesiastical movement of education in the faith. But what are the basic traits of this education? What are the essential steps in Msgr Giussani's educational method? These have been expressed in the numerous writings dedicated by Msgr Giussani to the communication of an educational method connected with the Christian proposal today (see Bibliography of Selected Works, p. 179).

Formulation of the human problem

The human phenomenon, our life, by the very fact that it exists, poses the problem of the meaning of this existence. Humans are, in fact, the only point in nature where the problem of the ultimate sense of existence is consciously posed, even if only as a confused question.

To verify any proposal, including the Christian one, humans have to start with their own authentic experience, in its completeness and genuineness, without partiality or confusion. We have authentic experience when the things that we feel or that happen to us are submitted to our judgment through comparison with that series of ultimate needs and "evidence" that make up the human heart and define its religious sense (the desire for happiness, truth, justice, beauty, ultimate and comprehensive meaning).

The encounter between these needs and "evidence" and the circumstances of life activates in individuals the dynamic of reason.

The nature of reason, then, is to be an opening to the real, to be a dynamic that, faced with an object, recognizes, even after the most thorough analysis, that there is something mysterious that escapes our understanding. Reason, faithful to its nature, opening to reality, questioning its meaning and recognizing the Mystery as the ultimate horizon of everything, "coincides" with that religious sense that Giovanni Battista Montini defined in 1957 as the "synthesis of the spirit."

The value of tradition and the way to approach it
The premise for an authentic human experience is to not cut out any of the factors making it up. In order to educate, it is thus necessary primarily to propose tradition as the sum of experiences and discoveries that determine in large measure the condition in which individuals find themselves and that, therefore, provide a first hypothesis for reading the present. Avoiding – or worse, obliterating – the relationship with tradition precludes the possibility of an authentic human experience.

But tradition, any tradition, can be proposed and thus encountered only in a living present. Otherwise it is reduced to an object of mere interest as something that is past, perhaps useful for specialized study, but inert as an influence on life. The encounter with tradition can happen only in the present, with an experience that lives the contents of that tradition in the present moment.

Thus, the encounter with the tradition of two thousand years of Christianity can also happen only in a point that lives its content and message in the present of today.

Authority and the critical sense
The human being develops in every dimension by following some authority. For the child this is the figure of parents; for every individual, whether aware of it or not, it is the figure – or figures – who inspire actions and establish the criteria by which they are done.

Nature has developed the method of authority as a norm for every true process of development. This does not have value in as much as it imposes certain criteria or methods for life and action, but in that it proposes the terms of the problem and suggests the proper hypothesis for facing it. Authority, in this sense, is an instrument for effective criticism: to educate, in effect, means to educate to a critical sense, to accustom students to face tradition, life, and its situations as a "problem" (from the Greek *pro-bállo*). This means facing life on the hypothesis that the criteria contained in the nature of the heart find most adequate. In this way the critical sense is not the same as doubt, which ends up paralyzing every search, but is the spring that continually launches individuals into the adventure of the real and makes them embrace all of life.

Christianity: the event of an encounter

A characteristic of reason is the category of possibility. Christianity is the announcement that an extraordinary and unignorable possibility has become a reality: the God who was sought and desired by humans in all ages and cultures, the Mystery toward whom man has cast the bridges of his imagination and prayer, became a man. He made himself available for an encounter, in history, at "a moment in time."[14] For this reason Christianity is not a "religion" among so many others: its nature is not that of a version of the unceasing search for God and the relationship with the Mystery from which everything comes forth. It presents itself as an event. The religious problem, with the Incarnation, has become a problem of history: is it true or not that Jesus is God-with-us?

Today, just as two thousand years ago, the encounter with an exceptional humanity, exceptional in that it corresponds in a unique way – as only God can do – to the expectations and desires of the heart, introduces us to the discovery of God made man. As for John and Andrew, so today the path of Christianity is simple: it is a question of following the attraction aroused by an encounter, to remain in that Presence.

But today where do we encounter Christ? Where does all this immense tradition of holiness, tenacity, tenderness, and charity aroused two thousand years ago by the event of Christ live, and how does it reach man today? Where, in a word, does that event continue to exist and continue to change people? In the Church, in the communion of those who recognize him and in the midst of whom he has established that he is mysteriously but really present. In the small group of friends (in whatever sphere they are found) that bases its unity on the recognition of Christ in the communion of the Church is found the ultimate terminal, the gesture by which Christ reaches man and makes himself something that can be experienced.

Certainty and the commitment of one's freedom
Speaking to the 1998 session of Exercises of the Fraternity of CL in Rimini, Msgr. Giussani said: "Faith is

rational, in that it flourishes at the extreme boundary of the dynamic of reason like a flower of grace, to which man adheres with his freedom. And how can man commit his freedom to this flower, which cannot be understood as to its origin and manufacture? Adhering with one's own liberty means, for man, recognizing in all simplicity what his reason perceives as exceptional, with that certain immediacy, as happens for the irrefutable and indestructible evidence of factors and moments of reality, just as they enter onto the horizon of one's own personality." In fact, just as we consider it reasonable to believe those who love us even if love cannot be measured, and as we find it perfectly rational to believe those who testify to any event – unless there are well-founded reasons for suspicion – thus also faith in the fact of Jesus who died and rose again is the fruit of a faith in the word of an innumerable series of witnesses, from then until now.

This type of certainty (moral certainty) is what the first disciples acquired about him in time, by staying with him, reading the signs of his power and love, verifying how his actions and words corresponded to the demands and evidences of their hearts.

The decisive factors in the acquisition of such a certainty of faith (like any moral certainty) are time and the commitment of freedom. To give time and to commit, also in actions and works, one's own freedom to the Christian proposal is the condition for verifying its reasonableness and adequacy for one's own existence.

Faith thus does not act on one's personal and social life simply as a "motive for inspiration" or an ideological preconception, alongside of or in opposition to other motives and ideologies, but as memory and the re-proposal of an event.

From whence the new morality arises
The authentic *morality* for the Christian becomes one with the act charged with affection with which he follows Christ and commits his freedom to that relationship. *To follow* him who has answered in an unexpected and complete way the expectations and the evidences of the heart: this change in morality does not arise from the respect due to rules or laws, but from the commitment of one's freedom and affection. From this urge that made St. Peter, the same man who had betrayed him three times, answer: "Yes, Lord, you know that I love you."[15]

Sanctuary of Our Lady of Caravaggio – Father Giussani
with a group of university students during
the Easter Triduum. Photo: A. Ascione

2

A BRIEF PROFILE OF LUIGI GIUSSANI

As is often the case with the biographies of founders of religious orders or movements, so too in the life of Msgr. Giussani it is not possible to trace one precise moment or situation in which he worked out a certain project or decided to create something new in the history of the Church. And also when one tries to identify this or that circumstance as the episode that explains what happens afterwards, one realizes that this or that episode assumes a more than ephemeral consistency from the fact that it was lived by a person who was already mysteriously predisposed to the task assigned to him by the Holy Spirit.

In conclusion, not even the sum of all that happened to Msgr. Giussani in his life at home, in the seminary, or in the various situations that he traversed is sufficient to "explain" the birth of a movement from this person. The gift of the Holy Spirit, or charism, introduces in this sense a value that at the same time augments and transfigures even the contingent circumstances in which the personality and temperament of the founder of a movement like CL were formed.

"I do not feel like a founder," Msgr. Giussani has written and repeats often, "for my whole life I have simply tried to live the Catholic faith as it was communicated to me by my mother and my teachers in the seminary."

Luigi Giussani was born in 1922 in Desio, a small town near Milan. His mother, Angela, gave him his first daily introduction to the faith. His father, Beniamino, a member of an artistically talented family, a carver and restorer of wood, spurred the young Luigi always to ask why, to seek the reason for things. Msgr. Giussani has often recalled episodes from his family life, signs of an atmosphere of great respect for persons and of an active education to keep alive the true dimensions of the heart and reason. For example, the episode when, still a young child, he and his mother were walking in the pale light of dawn to morning Mass, and his mother's sudden soft exclamation at the sight of the last star fading in the growing morning light, "How beautiful the world is, and how great is God!" Or the great love of his father, a Socialist anarchist, for music, a passion that led him not only to try to soften the impact of difficult moments in the family by singing famous arias, but also to prefer to the few comforts affordable in a modest economic situation the custom of inviting musicians home with him on Sunday afternoon so as to hear music played live.

At a very young age Luigi Giussani entered the diocesan seminary of Milan, continuing his studies and finally completing them at the theological school of Venegono under the guidance of masters like Gaetano Corti, Giovanni Colombo, Carlo Colombo, and Carlo Figini.

Besides the cultural training it offered, and his relationships of true esteem and great humanity with some of his masters, Venegono represented for Msgr. Giussani a very important environment for the experience of the company of some "colleagues," like Enrico Manfredini – the future archbishop of Bologna – in the common discovery of the value of a vocation, a value that is enacted in the world and for the world.

These were years of intense study and great discoveries, such as reading Leopardi, Msgr. Giussani recounts, as an accompaniment to meditation after the Eucharist. The conviction grew in him in those years that the summit of every human genius (however expressed) is the prophecy, sometimes unaware, of the coming of Christ. Thus he happened to read Leopardi's hymn *Alla sua donna [To his Woman]* as a sort of introduction to the prologue to the Gospel of St. John, and to recognize in Beethoven and Donizetti vivid expressions of the eternal religious sense of man.

From that moment, reference to the fact that truth is recognized by the beauty in which it manifests itself would always be part of the movement's educational method. One can see in the history of CL a privileged place given to aesthetics, in the most profound, Thomist sense of the term, compared to an insistence on an ethical referent. From the time of his years in the seminary and as a theology student, Msgr. Giussani learned that the aesthetic and ethical sense both arise from a correct and impassioned clarity concerning ontology, and that a lively aesthetic sense is the first sign of this, as shown by the healthiest Catholic as well as the Orthodox tradition.

Observance of discipline and order in seminary life became united with the strength of a temperament that in his dialogue with his superiors and the initiatives of his companions stood out for its vivacity and keenness. For example, he promoted together with some fellow students an internal newsletter, called *Studium Christi*,[16] with the intention of making of it a kind of organ for a study group dedicated to discovering the centrality of Christ in each subject that they studied.

After ordination, Father Giussani devoted himself to teaching at the seminary in Venegono. In those years he specialized in the study of Eastern theology (especially of the Slavophiles), American Protestant theology, and the pursuit of the rational motivations for adhesion to faith and the Church.

In the middle of the Fifties, he left seminary teaching for high schools. For ten years, from 1954 to 1964, he taught at the G. Berchet classical high school in Milan. In those same years he began a work of study and publicity aimed at drawing attention both inside and outside the Church to the problem of education. Among other activities, he wrote the entry on "Education" for the Catholic Encyclopedia.

These were the years of the birth and dissemination of GS (*Gioventù Studentesca*, Student Youth), and Msgr. Giussani was directly involved in leading the communities.

From 1964 to 1990 he occupied the chair of Introductory Theology at the Università Cattolica del Sacro

Cuore in Milan. On more than one occasion he was sent by his superiors to the United States for periods of study. In particular, in 1966 he spent some months in the States to further his study of American Protestant theology.

Today he heads the Communion and Liberation movement and is president of its General Council (commonly called the "Center").

He is also president of the Central Diaconia, the administrative organ of the Fraternity of Communion and Liberation, an association recognized by the Pontifical Council for the Laity in 1982.

Finally, he fosters and guides the experience of the *Memores Domini*, a lay association, also recognized by the Pontifical Council for the Laity (1988), which unites members of CL who have made the choice to consecrate their lives to God in virginity (on these two associations, cf. 5.1 and 5.2).

He is a councillor for the Congregation for the Clergy and the Pontifical Council for the Laity.

He was named Monsignor by Pope John Paul II in 1983, with the title of Honorary Prelate to His Holiness.

In 1995 he was awarded the International Catholic Culture Prize.

He is the author of numerous essays (see the Bibliography of Selected Works, p. 179), which have provided the basis for the formation of hundreds of thousands of young people and adults.

A FEW WORDS OF HISTORY

3.1. "HAS THE CHURCH FAILED MANKIND, OR HAS MANKIND FAILED THE CHURCH?" (T.S. ELIOT)

Recently, in an article in *L'Osservatore Romano*, Msgr. Giussani wrote: "What enlivens us is love for our humanity, that is, for the expectation of fulfillment that every man feels."[17]

In tracing the origins of the CL movement, we must note at the outset that Msgr. Giussani has always said he was aware of the existence of something which only much later would be called a "movement," because of the results and unexpected fruits that his call had generated in some young people with whom he was involved. It could be said, in fact, that the only "program" that guided Msgr. Giussani in his choice to enter high school teaching was that of proposing Christianity as the answer to the needs of the reason and experience of everyone and especially of young people.

He recounts, in this sense, that his decision to ask his superiors to assign him to teaching (abandoning, as mentioned above, a promising career as professional theologian) was due to episodes like the following.

It was 1954. During a train journey from Milan to the Adriatic Riviera, approaching some young people in his same compartment, he was shocked by the ignorance and the detached, scornful way with which these young people treated the questions of faith and the Church which had come up in their conversation. This dialogue documented the prophetic question which T.S. Eliot asked in the mid-Thirties in his "Choruses from 'The Rock'": "Has the Church failed mankind or has mankind failed the Church?"[18]

What struck Msgr. Giussani in this dialogue in the train was not so much their ignorance of catechism (at the time still quite widespread), but a more general and profound ignorance about the nature and essence itself of Christianity as an event that involves and transforms one's life.

Assigned to teaching at the G. Berchet classical high school in Milan, Msgr. Giussani very soon came up against what – under the guise of formal obeisance to Catholicism and a flourishing world of Catholic associations – was the true reality. That is to say, reality as it appeared to one who climbed the steps to the school with the hope that in every sphere the glory of Christ be experienced. In the spheres where people's life took place – in school, for example – there was practically no trace of the presence of Christians. While other groups of politically active young people were quite visible, and while a secular strategy of occupation of teaching positions and cultural hegemony was taking shape, there were no proposals or positions arising from the Christian experience in those spheres in which the prevailing outlook was inspired by the dogmas of secularism – those "dogmas" which say that there is no God, or if there is one, he has nothing to do with our lives. A Christian tradition followed only passively by this time – and thus perceptible only in certain references to morality or in some external manifestations of traditional associations – yielded to a present in which the Christian proposal was essentially irrelevant.

Msgr. Giussani intuited that it was necessary to re-propose the Christian experience by showing, especially to young people, that it answered the authentic needs of the reason and heart of every person. Already in an essay of 1955 ("Risposte cristiane ai problemi dei giovani" [Christian answers to the problems of young people]), published in an Azione Cattolica [Catholic Action] youth magazine, the term "movement" appears to indicate something that is activated in one's personality by the encounter with Christ. He was not the only person who understood in those years how real was the danger – which became much clearer in subsequent decades – that the Church might lose every ability to offer persuasive proposals to young people. But Msgr. Giussani set immediately to work to make the synthesis of the Christian proposal a reality, the one contained in Jesus' words: "And everyone who has given up … for the sake of my name will receive a hundred times more, and will inherit eternal life."[19]

3.2. THE RATIONALITY OF FAITH

Msgr. Giussani's special insistence on the hundredfold is translated into a proposal with pedagogical and practical characteristics that are often called original. In reality, Father Giussani has stated more than once that he did not "invent" anything, but only re-proposed what he himself had found reasonable in the teaching of his parents and teachers. These characteristics were made public in several articles and in the first three programmatic booklets of the movement,[20] which were a compendium of notes taken by his students during lessons at school or in group meetings.

The center of Msgr. Giussani's educational concern is the proposal of the reasonableness of faith. The founder of CL has often recalled the discussion he had about this subject on the very first day of school. As soon as he walked into class (First year, Section E, at Berchet high school), from the back of the room a hand was raised, and a boy said: "Professor, there's no point in your coming here and talking to us about religion. To talk, you have to use your reason, and faith and reason are like two oblique lines, they will never meet. One can say one thing and the other say the opposite."

Msgr. Giussani faced that objection, first asking the students if they had any idea what faith was, and then fast on the heels of that, asking what reason was for them. Not getting an answer, in the interval between classes he involved a philosophy teacher in the discussion, as it was probably his formulation which was at

The entrance to the Berchet High School in Milan,
where Father Giussani taught religion and where
the movement was born in 1954.

the origin of that separation and opposition between faith and reason.

Father Giussani recounts: "I said to him: 'Professor, these students use words whose meaning they don't know, and they use them to give opinions.' And I told him about the episode. He replied: 'They are right.' 'But what,' I said to him, 'you too?' And he said, 'The Second Council of Orange states that faith and reason are opposites of each other.' But I answered him: 'Look, I have taught theology for a while, but I really do not recall that this is something that is taught to seminarians. However, you who consider yourself an historian should know that a passage from a speech, a page of a book, a statement, must be judged, to find the meaning of their words, in terms of the climate of awareness and mentality dominant in their given epoch.' Since I had to go and the class was crowding all around to listen to what we were saying, and I wanted to leave the students with something definite, I said to the professor: 'Listen, professor, I swear to you that you are standing in front of me. Is this rational or not?' He answered, "Yes, because it is evident to you.' 'Well, I swear to you and state with equal certainty that America exists, even if I have never seen it and never will! (I was sure, then, that I would never see it, when instead I would go there many, too many times). I tell you that America exists, above and beyond the fact that I have seen it or could see it tomorrow. According to you, is it rational to say this or not?' And he preferred to remain loyal to his secular view of reason and said: 'No, it is not rational.' 'There, kids,' I exclaimed, 'the difference between me and your professor does not lie in the fact that I believe and he doesn't, the difference is not that I believe and you don't. But it is the fact that I have a concept of reason for which America exists, even if I have never seen it or measured it, for me it is reasonable to affirm its existence, and for him not.' Thus I introduced the concept of moral certainty, on which the reasonableness of faith is based."

If faith had no relationship with rationality, it could not have a real space in our lives, because man typically lives by rationality.

On the proposal of reason seen as a window open onto reality, on the call thus to live every aspect of reality according to its ultimate nature as a *sign* (we must admit that everything, in fact, even what has been most definitively investigated and known, refers to something else, to a "vanishing point") and on the call to be on guard against every reduction of reason to a mere instrument of measuring and taking hold of the real, Msgr. Giussani concentrated his teaching and actions at school.

With the notion of "religious sense," Msgr. Giussani aimed at indicating to his students that level of elementary needs and evidences of the heart, that series of ultimate questions that constitute and sustain the correct dynamic of the human heart and reason. Christianity is proposed once more as an historic event, a Fact that responds in a surprising and complete way to these needs, that "corresponds" more than any other proposal to the nature of reason. Or, more clearly, that corresponds to that unity of affection and reason given by the need for beauty, truth, and right, which the Bible calls the human "heart."

All this, according to Msgr. Giussani's insight, could not manifest itself solely in parish life or within the limits of a Catholic association, but had to be proposed as a hypothesis of work and presence in one's *environment*. This term, within CL, indicates any circumstance in which a person finds himself, and above all the one which for duration or importance contributes most to forming the personality. For young people this, of course, is school.

During a school assembly, one of the students whom Msgr. Giussani had earlier asked what was the meaning and visibility of his being Christian raised his hand and started out by saying, "We Catholics ..."; this was the first real confirmation that something *new* had been born. It was not a new theory about Christianity, but a new *experience*, here and now, of the Event handed down by tradition.

It is no coincidence that Msgr. Giussani's first writing proposing an orderly presentation of the guiding ideas and GS way of life is entitled *Riflessioni sopra un'esperienza* [Reflections on an Experience], published in 1959 with the *imprimatur* of Msgr. Figini, the austere ecclesiastical censor of the diocese of Milan. This little book is made up in large part of a reworking of the notes taken by students during the lessons on Christianity taught by Msgr. Giussani on Sunday mornings in the quarters of Catholic Action. For many young people, the encounter with Msgr. Giussani meant the discovery of a "school," of an educational group, which communicated an adequate Christian proposal.

3.3. EVERYTHING ALREADY THERE IN THE BEGINNING

From this point of view it is thus correct to set the year 1954, before Msgr. Giussani began teaching at Berchet, as the beginning of CL's life.

In the conversation entitled "How a Movement is Born," published in the appendix to this book, he affirms: "I still remember perfectly the day, so important for my life, when I walked up the four steps to the school's entrance for the first time. I was saying to myself: 'I am coming here to give these young people what was given to me.' I say this because that was *the only reason* we have done what we have done and why we will continue to do it as long as God allows us to: *that they should know Him*, that people know Christ."[21]

The *proprium* of the experience and charism of the movement is already completely present in these conversations and in the way the first students gathered around the young priest, struck by what he offered them.

But, as we said above, the young Father Giussani did not have in mind founding anything new. It was his intention to breathe new life into the Catholic asso-

ciations already existing. For this reason, for a while
Father Giussani's young friends and he himself considered themselves part of *Gioventù Studentesca* [Stu-
dent Youth], one of the youth groups of Catholic
Action. Only later, as Msgr. Giussani's educational
method became clearer and because of some misunderstandings, also in church circles, about the rapid
spread throughout Italy of the groups who saw him as
their guide, did they separate from the others.

Above and beyond the contestations and problems
that Msgr. Giussani encountered, we should recall
here also the support that the burgeoning experience
of GS-CL found in some authoritative men of the
Church, among them Cardinal G.B. Montini, at the
time Archbishop of Milan and later Pope Paul VI.
Although he confessed he did not understand completely Msgr. Giussani's methods (just think that Giussani was the first, within Catholic Action, to gather
together boys and girls, up to that time kept separate,
and to use vacation time as the perfect moment for education), he never failed to encourage Giussani's attempts, impressed by the results they were obtaining.
The future Pope wrote in a letter in February 1962 that
he did not want "to be silent about the pleasure and
consolation brought to my soul by such spiritual and
moral rectitude, and to all our Catholic world." In this
letter Montini praised "the courageous and ideally
consistent attitude shown in recent scholastic and academic events by members of GS." Because of these results, obtained in situations in which those who called

themselves Catholics were subjected to scorn and exclusion, Cardinal Montini always urged Msgr. Giussani to "go on in the same way." The aging Pope used these same words of encouragement many years later as he greeted Msgr. Giussani after Palm Sunday Mass in 1975.

In a short time, almost by "contagion," the GS experience spread throughout Italy, forming in its first ten years, up to 1965, a sort of movement created by the witness lived by students in the high schools and those they encountered as the first of them went on to the university. In its founder's intent, his GS was supposed to be a call to live with greater awareness a full Christian experience, developing the three dimensions intrinsic to the experience of faith: culture, charity, mission (cf. 4.4). In 1961, a GS *Note* was entitled: *GS is a Proposal of a Christian Experience*. In it we read, among other things: "GS works within the Church, from which it draws its certainties, its ideals, its very reason for being." And, in words that seem to foreshadow prophetically those of the council constitution *Gaudium et Spes* of December 1965: "GS participates in the anxieties, joys, problems, and mission of the Church."

From its beginnings, Msgr. Giussani's proposal concerning the value of authority as a principal factor of development for every authentic human experience (thus including the Christian one) and of communion as a method of witnessing to Christ, communicated to the participants in GS a vivid and aware sense of participation in the unity of the Church as the mysterious body of Christ. All this survives today, overcoming the trials of periods and spheres in which the dominant culture (and dominant even in "Catholic" circles) branded as absurd and backwards this sense of authority and communion.

To the early communities in schools that, starting from the first one at the Berchet high school, multiplied all over Milan (at the beginning of the 1960s GS already counted in the city several thousands of adherents) and through the rest of Italy, Msgr. Giussani proposed a method based on two "pillars": the "ray" and "initiatives."

3.4. THE "RAY"

In GS, the "ray" was an instrument by which the individual made a personal commitment to the proposal of community. This took the form of a weekly meeting in each school where there was a community, when GS members invited their friends to take part in a discussion whose outlines were prepared beforehand and presented as notes for discussion. As its name implies, the "ray" was not a closed structure, but was open to all, with the purpose of sharing and comparing experiences. The notes for discussion were suggested by passages from literature or the Bible or by current events; the discussion, coordinated and synthesized by a leader, was not, however, the chance to match one's wits or make subtle debating points. Everyone was invited to communicate his or her self, by recounting

Varigotti – Students' week: the "ray" at the tower.
Photo: Elio Ciol

and comparing one's own experience. Anyone could participate freely in these meetings.

As CL life developed, the moments of assembly, catechism, and discussion tended to preserve these basic characteristics of the "ray."

3.5. INITIATIVES

If the "ray" was the moment when each person was helped to compare his awareness and reality with the Christian proposal, the "initiatives" were an invitation to commit oneself and one's generosity to the ideal that had been encountered.

The Christian call, in fact, does not remove one from life, but makes one engage oneself with the totality of the factors making it up.

In this sense "initiatives" were occasions for praying together, cultural public debates, charitable activities (cf. 4.4.), vacations, the so-called "three days" – that is, moments of spiritual exercise and formation – trips, sports, theater; none of this was presented as obligatory to those who approached GS, but failure to participate would have meant remaining on the outside looking in at what the "ray" indicated as the enjoyment of an authentic Christian experience.

As it happened, GS life was immediately marked by a richness and variety of initiatives that, from the field of culture to that of expression, from social commitment to works of charity, enlivened the lives of its members and "infected" the schools and young people involved.

Milan 1964 – the departure of the first "Giessini"
(or students) for Brazil. Photo: Elio Ciol

Every circumstance, even a show at the Piccolo Teatro in Milan or a lesson at school, became an occasion to verify the Christian proposal and to form a judgement based on one's encounter with the Christian event.

Thus newsletters were spawned, occasions for cultural revision, debates and battles were started – even independently of the will of the GS members – like the one when Giussani's young people were the only ones to oppose the attempt to group all the identities and free initiative of school organizations under unified student associations. As early as that moment, GS grasped the importance for Catholics to fight every attempt to limit the freedom to teach and the freedom to educate. And not so much to preserve zones of truce or to cultivate through the institution of schools and the work of teachers one's own little Catholic garden, but to defend the primary and inalienable right of every truly free person to communicate himself and his own way of interpreting reality.

Along with initiatives born from the passion for liberty understood in its fullest sense, arose activities of charity and social awareness. And to share the universal mission of the Church in a concrete way, an original missionary initiative was started (in Brazil in 1962), for the first time totally self-supported by a community of young people.

Vacations, too, spent as part of the group or with one's family, were a special occasion for furthering and testing the Christian experience, confirming Msgr. Giussani's insight that it is how one spends one's free time that shows what type of experience orients one's interests as a person.

3.6. 1964–1969: CRISIS AND RENEWAL

GS's first ten years were thus marked by the unexpected flourishing of a Christian experience in the schools and in some universities.

In the years between 1965 and 1969 a crisis was played out within GS that, similarly to what happened in those years in the whole sphere of youth groups, especially Catholic ones, resulted in serious fractures and fragmentation. But the founder himself of GS has more than once pointed out that the crisis that hit the movement was not a *consequence* of the events of 1968, but a process that had been coming to a head for several years, starting in 1964.

The origins of this crisis should be sought in the fact that some of the leaders who found themselves at the helm of GS, at the moment in the fall of 1965 when Msgr. Giussani was offered a chair at the Università Cattolica in Milan, preferred to follow other paths than those traced out thus far by Giussani.

To sum it up briefly, we could say that those GS leaders, at a certain point, following impulses offered by encounters and readings not suggested by Msgr. Giussani, decided to place their emphasis on a reductive concept of faith. They followed certain theories which, although not lacking in positive elements, ended up considering Christianity as the occasion for social and political commitment, losing sight of the nature of the original event by which a divine factor entered into human history: Christ and the Church as the only possibility for true salvation.

This group, perhaps unawares, ended up accentuating a form of moral and social commitment, placing all hopes in man's sense of enterprise and in his initiatives. And they did not understand or want to understand any longer Msgr. Giussani's call to Christ and the Church. This call brought with it the need to preserve a unity with those in authority and within the community.

The crisis was long and painful. Already by 1966 two opposing groups had been formed. In 1968, finally, many of those GS leaders thought they had found in the ideals that hegemonized the so-called "student movement" the complete fulfillment of their commitment to faith. In their view, faith should become a personal motive for action and commitment, which would then be oriented according to the most appropriate "analyses" and most suitable lines for practice, above and beyond any concern for learning or for the Church. The Christian experience, for those who abandoned GS, no longer took the form of an integral religious event in which the dimension of social commitment is an inseparable consequence, but that of a "stimulus" to commitment.

GS thus split in two, suffering a serious hemorrhage.

The whole world of Catholic associations fell apart in those years. But for the young people who stayed with Msgr. Giussani, that crisis also marked the beginning of a new, clearer and more certain phase of their original experience.

In fact, this renewal under the name of Communion and Liberation can be considered one of the most unforeseeable ways in which the need for authenticity that in 1968 spurred the actions of so many young people, even under the too many ideological and political simplifications, found a path and a proposal that was truly adequate to the purpose.

Thus it happened that in the universities, that is, in the place where the hegemony of the so-called "revolutionary" movements did not tolerate the presence of anyone or anything which contested their ideas and ways of doing things, the Christian proposal initiated by Msgr. Giussani regained its form and clarity. The university students and adults who had stayed close to him found a reference point in the experience of the "Charles Péguy" center in Milan and in other similar centers in other cities in Italy where the movement had taken root. These centers, which came into being from 1965 on, acted as a gathering and reference point for persons and church groups also stimulated by the events taking place to assume clearly their own identity and their own responsibility in the Church of God in the world. From this starting point the groups of university students, first under the name of "Letter to Diognetus" and then from 1969 as "Communion and Liberation," soon resumed their presence and witness also in public.

In those same years immediately preceding the GS crisis and 1968, the movement had also reached a turning point, as unwanted as it was decisive.

If, in fact, up to 1964 the Gioventù Studentesca led by Msgr. Giussani, thanks to the benevolent and open attitude held by *Catholic Action*, was considered, even if not officially, as an aggregation within the overall framework of institutional associations, from the end of that year the space and possibility of a dialogue with the official lay organization of the Church in Italy were drastically reduced. This came about because at the top levels of *Catholic Action* the positions held by FUCI[22] prevailed.

Paradoxically, the experience of the so-called GS was recognized officially by Cardinal Colombo, Archbishop of Milan, as a "missionary movement in the environment of the two branches of Catholic Action"[23] just a few months after Father Giussani had had to give up directing it because of his university teaching.

"Our 'exodus from the institutions,'" Msgr. Giussani recounts, "was thus not the result of prejudice or presumptuousness, but the painful consequence of a history and of events that forced us to make a choice that we had neither expected nor prepared for. It was in any case a significant but not arbitrary change of direction, to which we were led by the just desire to protect our experience and its true nature by emancipating it from the narrowness of certain associational formulations whose pressure was becoming heavier and heavier."[24]

This new term "Communion and Liberation" contains within itself the reason and the resource of the new start: the Church is proposed as the place where the salvation inaugurated by Christ reaches its fulfillment. Redemption and salvation do not concern only the *beyond*, but have a fundamental reverberation in man's current historical condition. True liberation is not the fruit of some human enterprise, but is a new reality brought about by Christ. Building the Church – concretely: a Christian community in an environment – is the way to contribute to the process of the liberation of man, in whatever historical or social condition he finds himself.

Since 1969, then, the name CL has indicated the reality of the movement. Its presence in the universities acted as a flywheel to the creation of a presence which spread throughout Italy, and now that name began to be evident in areas also outside the schools and universities: in the world of work, above all.

3.7. THE 1970S:
FROM UTOPIA TO PRESENCE

The decade of the Seventies was marked by an assumption of responsibility on the part of the movement with regard to what was happening in Italian society.

Beginning in the early years of the decade, Italy underwent one after the other all the phases of that marked process of secularization and the hegemony of non-religious aspects of life whose early and shocking fruits Msgr. Giussani had discerned twenty years earlier in the classroom at Berchet high school.

CL appears in this context as an exception to the general submission of a large part of the so-called Catholic world to the dominant lines of secular culture, which became Marxist culture.

These are the years in which the "political" dimension towers over all the others, according to Marxist ideals that dominated the field of committed youth: the task of creating the conditions for man's liberation was assigned to the political sphere. In this context the accusation of "integralist" was often hurled in the direction of the young people in CL, to indicate, using a negative epithet, their *incomprehensible* insistence on seeing the Christian experience as the unifying criterion for an integral personal commitment, from the family to the workplace, from school to politics.

The three years from 1974 to 1976 were extremely intense ones for the movement. The referendum on divorce in 1974 marked a crucial, dramatic moment for the public presence of Catholics in Italy. The divisions which placed leading Catholic intellectuals against the bishops and people, the sense of a just battle fought on the wrong ground and with the wrong tools, the harsh aggression of the radical and secular press, favored by almost all the mass media, made of that moment a significant milestone which went far beyond that one particular object of legislation: Catholics realized brusquely that in Italy they were a minority. The fact that for many years they had held political power, including in key sectors like the Ministry of Education, had not prevented, and in fact at times had favored, the spread among the majority of an anti-Catholic outlook and culture. The first bitter fruits were being gathered of the lack of cultural creativity and the dualistic concept of World-Church, history-supernatural that had characterized the intellectual leadership of Catholic associations and a number of priests themselves from the Fifties onwards.

These were years when CL, also at the express invitation of the secretariat of the Italian Bishops Conference, at the time directed by Msgr. Bartoletti, committed all its energy to public action on the occasions of the referendum just mentioned and the local and national elections in the two following years. In those same years groups of Cattolici Popolari [People's Catholics] arose in the universities to present a unified Christian slate; in the first elections of collegial organs, despite the disruption and opposition of the far-left fringe, their candidates received a wide consensus, beating both the slates of the right and the left. In the fall of 1975, some CL members and other Catholics gave rise to the Movimento Popolare [People's Movement] as an instrument for a presence in society, against the elimination of Christians from the public arena, in favor of a renewal of action on the part of the Catholic movement.

All these and other motives contributed to making the nature of CL sometimes the object of confusion and of identification with social and political action.

What was more, while CL had been fighting, justifying its commitment with one sole purpose – defending the public impact of Christianity – the Catholic world had been characterized by a "diaspora" of many of its supporters toward Marxist parties, as well as by an interpretation within *Catholic Action* of the "religious choice" as a withdrawal from civic and social circumstances, and finally, by the choice on the part of numerous adepts of associations like ACLI[25] and Scouts to be active in leftist or far left groups.

Because of this choice to be committed and visible, CL was in those years a main target of the most ferocious anti-Catholic attacks, as well as the object of hundreds of acts of violence on the part of far left and far right groups, up to the escalation in the early months of 1977, when 120 attacks on persons or centers of CL were counted throughout all of Italy. This public "exposure" contributed, as said above, to arousing, on one side, in many observers a certain amount of confusion about the true nature of the movement, but on the other it persuaded others that such courage in going "against the current" and defending even at the cost of physical harm and personal slander the freedom of presence and expression of Catholics, and thus of everyone, could only arise from an authentic human and religious experience.

In March 1975, Pope Paul VI celebrated a Mass in Rome for the young people whom he had invited for Palm Sunday. At the end of the service he unexpectedly called for Msgr. Giussani. After an initial moment of surprise and embarrassment (Giussani was about to give the pyx he was holding to an even more astounded Swiss Guard in full uniform), Msgr. Giussani came forward, to hear the pope say: "This is the road, Father Giussani. Go right ahead in the same way," the same words that, as a Cardinal, Montini had said to him in the early years of GS. Looking out over St. Peter's Square, Pope Paul had probably realized that besides the 17,000 CL members, very few others had accepted his invitation. In those same years, the Pope had commented with both clear-sightedness and bitterness: "one could almost say that through some mysterious – no, it's not mysterious – fissure, the smoke of Satan has entered into the temple of God. There is doubt, there is uncertainty … We thought that after Vatican Council II a day of sunshine would have come for the history of the Church. And instead we have had a day of clouds and storm, of darkness, and of searching and uncertainty, it is difficult to impart the joy of communion."[26]

The Cardinal Vicar of Rome, Ugo Poletti, condemning episodes of aggression suffered by some CL young people a month earlier, had expressed his gratitude for the movement's commitment. And Paul VI, addressing a group of CL university students from Florence during his general audience of 28 December 1977, had said: "We thank you for the courageous, strong, and steadfast witness that you are giving in this particularly tumultuous moment, disturbed by certain torments and misunderstandings that surround you. Be happy, be faithful, be strong, and be glad to spread around you the testimony that the Christian faith is strong, is happy, is beautiful, and can truly transform in love and with love the society in which it finds itself."

In the course of those years, Father Giussani intervened on numerous occasions to support and correct his young followers, exposed as they were to the risks and the effort of a public commitment of those dimensions. In particular, he intervened on several occasions to remind the movement's leaders not to think that the nature and purpose of CL was to fight back, blow by blow, the enormous series of emergencies, provocations, and challenges arising from their environment and those around them who were pursuing ideological and political agendas of various kinds. It was not a case, according to Msgr. Giussani, of carrying forward a social and political program opposite and alternative to other projects. Faith should not be the base on which to build an ideology that, like all ideologies, tends to fulfill itself as a "hegemony" in society and the spheres in which it has an influence. "In 1954," recalled Father Giussani in 1976, addressing his university students who were exhausted by their numerous public commitments, "we did not go into the schools looking for an alternative project for the school; we went in aware that we were bringing something that saves man also in the school, which makes man real and authenticates the search for the truth, that is, Christ in our unity. Our purpose was *presence*."[27] Presence, or the reoccurrence of the same event of salvation as two thousand years ago, through a converted witness.

The call of 1976, which marked a new beginning, was healthy for the life and development of the movement. It became clearer that, within the great number of initiatives and with the assumption of social and civic responsibilities, love for the presence of Christ witnessed by brotherly unity acts more profoundly than the search for a political or social result, and that this is a consequence.

In the meantime, the movement grew in numbers and developed also internally.

From the middle of the 1970s the use spread of the "School of Community" as a central moment and source of all the life of the movement, while, especially among the CL members who had graduated from the university and entered the world as adults, the necessity was increasingly felt to feel more concretely the experience of an authentic Christian fraternity (cf. 5.1).

3.8. THE 1980S: A NAIVE BOLDNESS AND A MISSION

When in October of 1978, after the brief pontificate of John Paul I, the "unknown" Karol Wojtyla was elected, the one to furnish the astounded and somewhat perplexed television journalists with a profile of the new Pope was Father Francesco Ricci, one of Msgr. Giussani's earliest companions on the road he had taken. Ricci, a tireless traveler and disseminator of the movement in numerous countries throughout the world, including Poland, had already had occasion to know and admire the Cardinal of Cracow.

Three months after his election, John Paul II received Msgr. Giussani in a private audience. The founder of CL came out of it convinced that "serving this pope" coincided with the pursuit of the movement's vocation.

The close connection between CL and Pope John Paul II is not based, as has often been said, solely on character traits or external coincidences: the root lies in a shared perception of the nature of faith and the culture that arises from it.

A GS document of 1960 defines the concept that is born from faith: "Christ is the center of personal and historical experience, just as he is the key to all of reality." After almost twenty years, John Paul II would begin his first encyclical, *Redemptor hominis*, with similar words: "Man's Redeemer, Jesus Christ, is the center of the cosmos and of history."[28]

With the papacy of John Paul II, all the vast and varied range of movements received new impulse and prestige. The Pope himself, meeting the movements' leaders at Castelgandolfo, affirmed in a brief but incisive talk that "the Church itself is a movement."

Probably the most important effect of the encounter between John Paul II and the CL movement is CL's realization of the value of its *charism* (cf. 1.2) within a full ecclesiology of communion, as can be read in the teachings of the Church.

During the 1980s we thus see a more aware return to that "naive boldness" that had characterized, according to Msgr. Giussani, the beginnings of the experience of GS as a Christian movement in an environment.

In 1982 the Pontifical Council for the Laity recognized as an association under Canon Law the Fraternity of Communion and Liberation, which is the most mature and aware adult level of the movement experience (cf. 5.1).

This was followed in 1988 by the Pontifical Council for the Laity's recognition of *Memores Domini*, a group which arose within Communion and Liberation, whose members consecrate themselves to God through the promise of obedience, poverty and chastity (cf. 5.2).

These are two important events, which clarify definitively what Msgr. Giussani has always maintained: the coincidence of the movement experience with the nature and aims of the mission of the Church, under the sign of a recognized ecclesial reality, approved and supported by the Holy See.

Beginning in the 1980s, besides the flourishing of charitable initiatives and social and cultural works on the part of CL members, there was an enormous and unplanned rise of communities in numerous foreign countries. Already in many of these countries, dating back to the 1960s, core groups of CL adherents had been present (in Brazil, Poland, Uganda, Argentina, Chile ...), but now the movement seemed to find a new missionary impulse. Among the facts that mark this surge, particularly significant is the meeting with Pope John Paul II on the thirtieth anniversary of the birth of the movement: "Go out into all the world as bearers of the truth, beauty, and peace that are encountered in Christ the Redeemer," he said to the CL members in attendance.

In that speech, given on 29 September 1984, John Paul II traced out the badge of the charism of CL and its function within the mission of the Church.

On that occasion, furthermore, the Pope (as he also did on a later occasion) fixed in these terms the contents of the faith: "We believe in Christ who died and rose again, in Christ who is present here and now, who alone can change and does change, by transforming them, man and the world."

In another passage, the Pope answered the question which all the actions of CL try to solve, that is, where in the present this relationship with Christ and the change it brings about can take place. "Continue in commitment on this path," said the Pope, "so that also through you the Church can be ever more the place of the redeemed existence of man." "The Christian experience," John Paul II added, "understood and lived in this way, generates a presence that sets in every human circumstance the Church as the place where the *event* of Christ, 'a stumbling block to Jews and foolishness to Gentiles,' lives as the horizon filled with truth for man" (cf. Appendix, p. 134).

Rome, 29 September 1984 – Pope John Paul II
with Father Giussani on the occasion of the Papal
audience for the thirtieth anniversary of Communion
and Liberation. Photo: Felici

The Eighties found CL still on the front line, especially in the universities, of the battles for freedom and democracy. The time of the great and sometimes violent ideological confrontations now past, the ideals of individualism and indifference came forth, the natural children of those ideological diatribes. It was thus on the plane of concrete actions that the attachment to ideals was verified for adherents to CL, or so-called "ciellini". Hundreds of thousands of students knew the Christian experience because it was proposed by these young people who offered gratuitously to help entering freshmen find their way around and students to find housing and the services they needed.

The 1981 referendum which legalized the practice of abortion in Italy had confirmed, if there had still been any need to do so, that the position of the Church and Catholic culture had by this point only marginal influence on people's conscience.

In this context, marked still by diffidence within and without the Church, CL continued nonetheless to grow in the maturity of its presence.

After thirty years from its beginnings, the presence of Msgr. Giussani's "kids" was shown yet again to be sensitive to the most widespread needs (like the problem of unemployment, or the wish to educate children not only by the often depressing methods of the state schools) and most lively cultural questions.

In 1986 the young university graduates and adults in the movement, along with others – Catholics and non-Catholics alike – gave life to a free initiative of social presence within the framework of Catholic social doctrine and the Catholic movement tradition. This was the Compagnia delle Opere (Company of Works), which, in a constructive way, gradually took the place of the Movimento Popolare (which ceased activity in 1993), drained by the ambiguities and the harshness of the exhausting political struggle of those years.

Cooperatives arose, as did organizations for international aid and solidarity, and some journalists and cultural leaders created organs for information and debate (like the weekly *Il Sabato* and the monthly *30 Giorni*). Also in the political field, the presence of people who had grown up in CL began to take root in more personal and concrete terms.

3.9. TOWARD THE CELEBRATION OF THE GREAT JUBILEE: EDUCATION, FRATERNITY, AND WORKS

Outside of Italy there now exist communities which, due to the number of their participants and the maturity of their experience, have become important for the leadership of the movement; this is true of Spain, whose leaders are involved in the general direction of the movement. The presence already established during the Seventies (Brazil, Argentina, Chile, Uganda, Poland, Switzerland, Spain) reached dozens of other countries during the Eighties.

The movement's missionary vocation is contained in the "DNA" of the initial GS experience. Some of the first gatherings proposed by Father Giussani to his "kids," in fact, had as theme the opening to the dimensions of the whole world which is an integral part of every authentic Catholic experience. A memorable occasion was the meeting entitled *Vivere le dimensioni del mondo* ("Living the world's dimensions"), with the participation of Giorgio La Pira at the beginning of the 1960s.

From the beginning, the movement spread without organized plans or strategies. Just as it spread from Milan through the Romagna region by some of Msgr. Giussani's encounters and the vacations of early GS members on the Adriatric coast, so too in these years it arose in countries near and far (such as Mexico, Taiwan, Japan) for sometimes fortuitous reasons (a business trip, unexpected friendships and occasions for collaboration). Alongside these phenomena, as years passed the request became more pressing on the part of bishops and priests from all over the world for CL to send out priests and laypeople who had grown up in the movement.

The recent publication of Msgr. Giussani's basic writings by McGill-Queen's University Press and their presentation, organized by the Papal Nuncio, at the United Nations building in New York are a sign of the unforeseeable frontiers open to the movement.

In recent years, the presence of CL in society has become more specifically attuned to its educational, cultural, and social nature.

At a moment when, for various reasons, even politics and the confrontation of ideas seem to have lost their ability to involve people on a personal level, and in which, not only in Italy, some have presumed to disguise the struggle for power as a moral revolution, the movement is concentrating on the crisis at the root of all the social and political crises: the crisis in education.

Through the action of many committed adults in the schools (where the use of the old initials GS still continues) and as youth group leaders, CL today offers its contribution to keeping alive positive educational proposals in a society that seems at times definitively exhausted and emptied of all its urge to idealism. And, through the social and also political action of members and friends of the movement, the same question continues to be raised that marked one of the earliest battles of GS from the 1950s: the right to freedom of education. "You can make us go around naked, but at least leave us the freedom to educate," was and is one of CL's slogans. This freedom, in fact, encompasses all the true freedoms that a non-oppressive society must guarantee and value: from free enterprise to freedom of association.

But the idea itself of freedom, like that of reason, seems today to be among those most distorted and misunderstood. Just recently Msgr. Giussani noted: "The first problem that we notice in modern culture is that we feel like beggars of the idea of reason, since it is as though no one any more had a concept of reason, and we understand – on the contrary – that faith needs man to be reasonable so that he can recognize the grace of the coming of God with us."[29]

In particular, in the face of a culture that tends to make positions founded on pantheism or nihilism pass as reasonable, CL calls us back to a concept of reason understood as an opening to reality, with a privileged position given to the "fact" over what is a preconception or ideological reduction. As we read in a text that was one of the first to be adopted by GS, recommended by Msgr. Giussani, "'reasonable' indicates someone who subjects reason to experience."[30] This emphasis given to experience and the emerging within experience of events as the law of reality has led CL to fight, even in Catholic spheres, against every reduction of Christianity and the figure of Christ to "morality" or a "word" or a pure disincarnate abstraction.

Also in polemic with those whom a poet and writer dear to CL, Charles Péguy, called "opposing bands of curates, clerics, and anti-clerics," the movement, through its publications and the free, responsible action of committed lay people in the mass media and in publishing and cultural concerns, has reaffirmed the centrality of the method of the Incarnation against every spiritualistic, gnostic, or Pelagian reduction, and, on the opposite side, against every dualistic separation between what regards the temporal and what belongs to faith.

It is true that the reduction that Christianity is suffering today, often passed off as one of the possible forms of philanthropy or as an abstruse way toward moral perfection, even sometimes under a formal obeisance toward the Pope and the Church, is one of the gravest in history. Whoever has had his life touched and transformed by the encounter with an experience of reasonable faith and has discovered the unmatchable attraction of the figure of Christ cannot but react: also by becoming active in society for the construction of works and realities that witness concretely to an attention to need and the expression of talents. "Pour se poser Il s'oppose," (*to propose, He opposes*) is one of the sayings attributed to Christ that is most often repeated in CL.

From the point of view of the movement, these most recent years have been marked by an increasing centrality of the catechism offered by the "School of Community" and by the growth of Fraternity groups, that is, groups of adults spontaneously coming together to commit their lives in a desire for holiness through a "rule" of personal ascesis, a lived communion, and charity (cf. 5.1).

CL's contribution on the threshold of the Jubilee Year is thus distinguished by three words: education, fraternity, and works. These are the three factors in which currently and concretely CL spends its energy with the aim of contributing to the human glory of Christ in history.

As Father Giussani has said: "The rabbi of Rome, Elio Toaff, wrote in a recent book: 'The Messianic epoch is precisely the opposite of what Christianity wants: we Jews want to bring God back to earth and not man into heaven. We do not give the kingdom of heaven to men, but we want God to return to reign on earth.'[31] When I read this I jumped in my chair! This is exactly the nature of the charism with which we have perceived and felt Christianity, because Christianity is 'God on earth,' and our work has as its goal, all our life has as its goal Christ's glory, the glory of Christ the man, of the God-man Christ. Christ's glory is a temporal thing, in time, in space, in history, of history, on this side of the ultimate boundary, because on the other side He takes care of His own glory: it coincides with the eternal beyond, but if on this side I do not serve him, his glory is lessened."[32]

Rimini 1998 – The Spiritual Exercises of the Fraternity
of Communion and Liberation on the theme "The Miracle
of Change." Twenty-one thousand people in Italy took
part as did many others via satellite to forty-four countries
of the world. Photo: R. Masi

4

A LIFE EVENT

4.1. FREE ADHESION

Those who come into contact with the life of CL members are surprised, partly as a result of slogans circulating in the mass media and the ridicule to which they are often exposed, to learn that life in CL is a normal life, in the sense that adhesion to the movement does not involve any special obligations or strange customs.

One of its characteristics, to which the movement has always held fast and which distinguishes it immediately from traditional Catholic associations, is the absence of any form of application for membership. Anyone who wants to belong to CL can do so without asking permission from anyone else.

The life of the movement tends to elude what Cardinal Ratzinger has called the risk of "self-occupation" on the part of numerous institutions and elements in the Church. That is to say, the call which goes out to CL adherents insists on the "missionary" vocation at the movement's origin, rather than the creation of organs and organizational structures whose activity takes place within the movement itself or the Church.

4.2. FUNDAMENTAL GESTURES

School of Community

Besides the invitation to prayer and regular practice of the sacraments addressed to every Catholic, Father Giussani's movement invites its members and anyone else who wishes to participate in a moment, usually weekly, of discussion and catechism. In the beginning, we have noted, in Gioventù Studentesca life, this moment was called the "ray." From the mid-Seventies, while taking place in the same way (cf. 3.4), it changed its name to "School of Community." In fact, it aims at being a true school which, through the reading and discussion of texts indicated by the movement's Center, helps participants to come to a clearer understanding of the nature of the Christian fact and of the Church. The indicated texts usually come from Msgr. Giussani's writings or from the teachings of the Church.

School of Community is the usual moment for catechism and meeting together, for high school and university youth and for adults.

Following Father Giussani's outlines for all the community's actions from its beginnings, School of Community too is "public," something of value offered to everyone, in the sense that it is open to participation to all and is often publicly proposed in places of study or work.

Other acts of fundamental importance in CL life are charitable work, vacation, and reading (or cultural work).

Charitable work

This term indicates the performance of an act of charity or of unpaid dedication to charitable work at regular intervals. This regularity and the fact that the acts are not carried out with the aim of responding in an exhaustive way to a need, serve to recall in everyday life that the "law" most suited to life is the free giving brought by Christianity (cf. 4.4).

Vacation

Vacations, especially those taken together in some place in the mountains, have always been one of the most important moments for discovering the joy of Christian companionship and the attitude of wonder and respect to which it educates in the face of the reality of creation.

From the beginning, the first "observers" were astounded at how Father Giussani would take even large groups of young people to the mountains for vacations, making of these moments (as opposed to what usually happens with school groups or even with many Catholic associations) an occasion of joyous and orderly companionship and of a markedly Christian proposal.

And, as we have already noted, it is during one's so-called free time that one also reveals the things one truly pays attention to and to what ideals one is dedicated.

These vacation times, whether lived in the group or within the individual family, are also a chance to offer the experience encountered in the movement to others.

Reading

Another of the ways in which CL educates its adherents to a critical sense, to a discovery of human dignity and the true facé of the Church, is an invitation to the reading of books (for example through the so-called "book of the month") and to cultural work, urging them not to neglect the value of beauty as it emerges in certain masterpieces of classical music, painting, and cinema. CL members have become familiar with and recognized as worthy of further study names like Dante, Leopardi, Pascoli, Ada Negri, Pasolini, Montale, Péguy, Eliot, Falco, Solov'ev, De Lubac, Dawson, Moeller, Mounier, along with Schubert, Beethoven, Mozart, Donizetti, and Giotto, Antelami, Masaccio, Caravaggio, and again Dreyer and other giants of literature and art.

Singing

One of the acts that marked the birth and has accompanied the development of Communion and Liberation is singing, especially group singing. Whether liturgical music, songs resulting from the experience of CL members (some of whom have been around the world) or songs taken from the popular repertory of other nations, attention to group singing is one of the distinguishing traits of CL meetings. In song the community expresses its unity in a synthetic and persuasive way, and the gladness and new awareness that arise from that unity.

Common fund

From the movement's beginnings, one of its most educational actions has been the so-called "common fund." This is a fund whose aim is the furthering of the movement's work through support of missionary, charitable, and cultural activities. Everyone gives freely to this fund, contributing monthly a percentage of income (at the beginning of the movement's history this was called the "tithe"). The purpose of this gesture is to witness to a communal concept of personal property and a growth in awareness of poverty as an evangelical virtue. The amount each one gives is not important, but what matters is the seriousness with which one fulfills this commitment that was freely made. It is this seriousness that permits each person to be educated to charity, to become truly aware of the fact that what one owns does not belong only to him, and that a personal budget has to take into consideration also the needs of others.

Litterae communionis – Tracce

Among the acts making up CL life is, if one could call it that, the communal editing of the movement's official magazine. *Litterae communionis – Tracce*, besides offering with every monthly issue articles and in-depth studies of current events and social issues, is the instrument through which the life of the movement is recounted.

An ample section devoted to letters shares with readers the testimony, problems, and challenges that arrive daily in a life of faith.

We have called these gestures "fundamental," but none of them is considered obligatory. The CL experience, in fact, more than aiming at a rigid definition of what is involved in adhesion to the movement, trusts in the communication of its fundamental steps, and thus the gestures which foster them, through the process of "osmosis" that takes place between those participating in a friendship that is not superficial.

As Prof. Nikolaus Lobkowicz, past president of the Catholic University of Eichstätt, has recently written: "It is no coincidence that friendship is one of the virtues that the movement founded by Father Giussani practices most joyously; a friendship offered to everyone encountered on one's path and that does not fail even if the friend takes a path that one cannot approve."[33]

4.3. PRAYER

One of CL's distinguishing traits is its attention to acts of personal and community prayer, also through the publication, with ecclesiastical *imprimatur*, of a *Book of Hours* reproducing part of the Breviary prayed by the universal Church, through attention to songs for the liturgy and the learning of hymns and canticles from tradition. This attention has led to the "invention" of a sort of vigil of preparation to the gestures made during Holy Week, made up in a powerfully evocative way of Bible readings, passages from the poetic works of Christian meditation by Charles Péguy, and choral and musical passages from the liturgical tradition and from the repertory of the greatest works inspired by religious moments, like Mozart's *Requiem* or Pergolesi's *Stabat Mater*.

The habit of reciting the *Angelus* or repeating particularly significant traditional ejaculatory prayers (like *Veni Sancte Spiritus, Veni per Mariam*) tends to generate in CL adherents a familiarity with prayer in its truest and simplest sense.

This is, in fact, the first expression of communion. It is the first fruit of an authentically experienced community life. It is not just the explicit action expressed in the group reciting of the Psalms or personal prayer. Prayer is the expression of a dependence on the Other that every reasonable and realistic person feels. Msgr. Giussani writes that "it is a need implicit in our nature to seek perfection and happiness ... Precisely because the network of our actions constitutes our attempt to pursue happiness, prayer, by reawakening understanding of the true road to this happiness, must tend to become a constant dimension of the active person. Jesus said, 'Pray without ceasing.' "[34]

4.4. THE THREE DIMENSIONS OF
EXPERIENCE: CULTURE, CHARITY, MISSION

Culture: a test of experience, political action, ecumenism
"A faith that does not become culture," stated John
Paul II in 1982, "is a faith that is not completely ac-
cepted, not totally thought out, not faithfully lived."[35]

In line with these words, the life of GS first and
then of CL has always been marked by a fertile cultural activity. This energy does not originate in an
emphasis on culture as an intellectual arrangement
or a scholarly study of topics of a religious nature or
connected with Christian life. On the contrary. The
cultural energy of CL, expressed in the hundreds of
types of initiatives undertaken by its founder and by
his followers under their own direct responsibility,
arises rather from a passion to verify the capacity of
the Christian faith to offer a more fertile and all-encompassing criterion for interpreting reality and
events. St. Paul's advice: "Test everything; retain
what is good,"[36] remains for CL the best definition of
cultural work: everything can be encountered and
compared taking as a criterion the clarity about man
brought by the Christian revelation, and using this
criterion, we can retain and give value to what is true
and good in everything.

Cultural work, then, coincides with a critical and
systematic awareness of reality as it arises from a
lived experience, and not from the application of a re-

ligious-type scheme to the interpretation of events and problems.

From the beginning Father Giussani's young people, subjected to a cultural and scholastic environment that, then as today, tends to marginalize the Christian event as a hypothesis for reading reality, engaged themselves in symposia, newsletters and the so-called "revision cards" in an effort to have their say in questions raised by their school lessons or current social and cultural events. Alongside these, authors, texts, and problems were rediscovered and proposed that had been censured or neglected by the prevailing cultural tendencies.

In this "school" individuals and groups grew up who then started or contributed to cultural initiatives of their own responsibility, on a national and international level, along with a myriad of undertakings, great and small, embracing both the joy of sharing experiences and the passion to communicate the *proprium* of the Christian event.

Thus there grew up, in and outside of Italy, hundreds of cultural centers, dozens of private schools, (often promoted by parents' cooperatives), publishing houses were started, journalistic and publishing activities realized, Institutes and Foundations on an academic level promoted, and international meetings (like the annual "Meeting for Friendship among Peoples" in Rimini) involving the most illustrious names in international culture and

Rimini, 29 August 1982 – John Paul II at the Meeting
for Friendship among Peoples. Photo: F. Brunetti

debating the most burning and authentic questions of
the present moment.

All this has attracted both benevolent and ill-inten-
tioned feelings to the movement, insofar as, above and
beyond the inevitable errors that the above-mentioned
work brings with it, observers feel a difficulty if not a
preclusion to considering the Christian identity as
bearer of an original judgment with regard to culture
and society. Those who, even within the so-called
Catholic world, see faith as something regarding questions "above the clouds" and not as a factor that intervenes in history and culture would prefer the
Christian community to stay out of questions beyond
the sacristy door.

a) Politics

In a committed Christian experience the political
dimension naturally descends from the cultural dimension. Political action, in fact, in the conception of
CL, is one of the fields in which a Christian is called
with greater responsibility and ideal generosity to
verify the unifying criterion that guides his existence
in the face of the problems posed by the life of society and institutions. It should thus not be surprising
that out of CL have come people engaged on various
levels, directly and under their own responsibility, in
political action.

In particular, what gives life to the Christian commitment in politics is defense of that highest good
which is freedom, a necessary condition so that man

can seek adequate answers to what his heart desires and his needs require. This freedom is too often threatened in modern times by the absolutist tendencies – manifest or hidden – of the State and of ideologies which see the State as the source of the rights of the individual and of free association. The political action typical of the person educated in the movement must tend, thus, to create the conditions so that the individual and society, in the sum of its activities of production, culture, and association, are not diminished or penalized by a statist view or by a position of privilege granted only to some for reasons of power. All of this, of course, in the clear awareness of what has been affirmed by Cardinal J. Ratzinger among others, which is that politics is the art of compromise.

In this sense, the battles that have involved not only single individuals but the entire movement, like that for the freedom of education and a condition of parity between state and private schools, or the broader one for respect of the principle of "subsidiarity," tend to create a unity between cultural and political action.

These, moreover, following the track established by the social doctrine of the Church, serve to verify to what extent that doctrine remains a dead letter or a pure pretext for an ambiguous "Christian inspiration" claimed by politicians and government figures, when it too is not subjected to the cultural test within the sphere of a lived experience of Christian community.

b) Culture, or ecumenism

In short, according to the terminology used by the early Christians who indicated the *oìkoumene* as the world that was the object of their mission, CL's concept of culture coincides with the most authentic sense of the term ecumenism. Ecumenism is not the search for a lowest common denominator between diverse experiences with the aim of justifying a tolerance that resembles, in fact, a lack of reciprocated love. Ecumenism as the true meaning of culture indicates the capacity to embrace even the most distant and different experience from one's own, by virtue of the fact that having encountered it by grace and not by one's own merit, one is able to recognize every glimmer of truth and to enhance it.

Charity: free giving as a law, the working of charity

One of the actions promoted by GS as early as 1958 was charity in the area of the "Bassa milanese". Every week, several hundred students went from Milan to its outskirts, called the "Bassa," where the living conditions of many families were close to the poverty line and social life was badly compromised. These students stayed there for several hours, playing with the children and organizing them, in accord with the local parish priests, in periods of reading instruction and catechism. They also tried to help the families meet their daily needs.

The charitable proposal, which from that moment has involved tens of thousands of young people and

adults in visits to the elderly and the sick, or in charitable acts toward the poor or people struck by calam-
ity, has always been clearly motivated. It is not a
question of performing philanthropic acts or claiming
to offer with these initiatives exhaustive answers to
needs that are often vast and complex, but of learning,
through faithfulness to an exemplary act, that the ultimate law of existence is charity, free giving. The habit
of treating everything gratuitously: this is what Christianity brought into the world, opposed to every attitude of egoistic possession.

Free giving is the law of Being. Man is asked, in
order to fulfill his own nature, to act in the image
and semblance of God. Free giving, the summit of
every moral ascesis, has thus become a word that
does not designate an impossible virtue, but something to make room for, a "small" habit capable of
bringing ferment and change into all the aspects of
life.

From this "school" of free giving has arisen in Italy
and throughout the world, through the free and responsible initiative of CL members or thanks to their
contribution, a dense network of large and small
charitable activities, in the most disparate fields:
from taking into the family persons in need to the
creation of real family-houses for difficult cases (drug
addicts, the mentally disturbed, persons with handicaps, AIDS patients, the terminally ill); from the creation of enterprises aimed at the insertion into the
work world of persons with handicaps to the founda-

tion of non-government agencies for projects of development and assistance in the poorer nations (for example, AVSI in Italy, recognized by the United Nations, and CESAL in Spain); from the constitution of foundations like the Food Bank (which provides daily sustenance to more than 500,000 poor people in Italy from the production surplus of medium and large industries) to the creation of Solidarity Centers to help unemployed young (and not so young) people find work; from assistance in juvenile prisons in Africa and Latin America to the simple economic support of families in need.

Since these are in very many cases works which unite a charitable purpose with a business-like organization, it could be said that these initiatives revive the tradition of the great works of charity that has marked the history of Christianity, adapted to current conditions and often under the aegis of what is called the non-profit sector. Also in this case, as in the case of culture, these developments are linked to the free initiative and the choice to make a commitment on the part of individuals or groups belonging to CL and do not involve the movement as such in the definition of their instruments or results.

Mission: a Catholic witness
The term mission underlines the most profound meaning of the word "Catholicity."

This dimension of Catholicity, that is to say of the validity of its proposal for man in every place and time and in every situation, is an integral part of a Christian education.

The GS experience was marked from the beginning by this "passion." GS youth were educated to a sense of mission also through attention to figures of missionaries working in distant and difficult places. Throughout its entire history, CL has contributed to the missionary work of leading personalities (from Marcello Candia to Msgr. Pirovano, from Father Lardo to Mother Theresa) or religious organizations or orders (the Pime Fathers, the Comboni Missionaries). But what counted most was the proposal made to these high school students to support entirely and responsibly (perhaps for the first time in Church history) a missionary action in Brazil, at Belo Horizonte in 1962. The mission in Brazil has a significance that goes well beyond the fact that with the departures of those twenty-year-olds the first seeds were sown of the movement's presence in Latin America: for the whole history of the movement that gesture has meant that there is no distinction between an invitation to a "ray" or School of Community meeting or an offer of companionship to a colleague, and the action of Christian proclamation carried out by the many missionaries, today also including representatives of CL, in difficult lands in Africa, Asia, or the Americas. It is the same universal mission of the Church, the same announcement.

A sense of mission in one's own sphere, the testimony to which the movement calls its members, are understood above all as the offer of one's time and talents to Christ, more than as the capacity for initiative or strategies for communication. Mission in one's own sphere does not come about because of intention or by showing how well one can do something, but by the simplicity with which one commits oneself completely to the attraction of the Christian event. In this sense, mission becomes the same as *presence*. The witness of a changed individual, and of a community life, documents the newness of the Christian event.

Under this profile, more than being concerned with its own dissemination, CL has always understood mission as service to the mission of the Church and as the possibility of a call to the Christian experience in every sphere of study or work in which its members are found, anywhere in the world.

4.5. STRUCTURE AND ORGANIZATION

The organizational structure of a movement like CL is elastic by nature. At its top is the General Council (commonly called the "Center") presided over by Msgr. Giussani and uniting the directors in Italy and abroad for every sphere – school, university, work, culture, etc. – in which the movement operates.

Each of these spheres is led by its own group of leaders. On the local level – national, regional, or city – the movement is guided by "diaconias," that is, groups of leaders available for service (from which their name derives) to the life of the community.

The leaders are chosen from among those who show the clearest awareness of the movement's aims and most generous witness and dedication of service to the community.

The activities of the movement are completely self-financed by its adherents through the "common fund."

The monthly magazine *Litterae communionis – Tracce* (cf. 4.2) is published in various languages by editorial committees cooperating with each other in various countries throughout the world.

FORMS OF COMMUNITY LIFE RESULTING FROM THE CL EXPERIENCE

There follows a brief outline of some of the types of life in community to which CL has given rise and which derive directly from its special charism.

5.1. THE FRATERNITY OF COMMUNION AND LIBERATION

This is the eminent group among those born from the movement, whose origins and aims it shares. It was recognized as a Lay Association under Canon Law on 11 February 1982. The decree of approval of the Fraternity's request for recognition reads that the Holy Father himself was "benevolently pleased to encourage the Pontifical Council for the Laity" that the recognition procedure have a positive outcome. The letter accompanying the decree, signed by Cardinal Opilio Rossi, recognizes that the Fraternity of CL's contribution to the Church in her work of evangelization is "of outstanding importance and pastoral urgency," especially in "distant" de-Christianized areas where "the basic principles of human life and social interchange are at stake." The ecclesiastical nature of the Association, the letter concludes, makes obvious its "full cooperation and communion with the Bishops, with at their head the supreme Pastor of the Church," down to the pastoral life of the diocese, to which it offers "its experience and contribution."

This recognition from the Pontifical Council for the Laity marked *de facto* approval of the educational experience of CL.

The first groups of "Fraternity" were formed around the mid-1970s at the initiative of some "ex-university" CL members who wanted to go more deeply into what it means to belong to the Church, also within the conditions of adult life and the responsibilities it brings, and by means of a communitary method.

Today the Fraternity counts over 38,000 men and women, who have made the decision to commit themselves to a way of life that supports the path to holiness, recognized as the true aim of existence. The life of the Fraternity normally takes place through the free formation of groups who consider that commitment as the reason for their friendship and sharing. Recent years have witnessed also in Italy and abroad the rise of Fraternity groups formed by diocesan priests (the first of these took the name of *Studium Christi*) who in this way intend to help each other go more deeply into their vocation and the accomplishment of their mission.

Belonging to the Fraternity involves a minimal rule of personal ascesis, daily prayer, participation in spiritual formation meetings including an annual period of spiritual exercises, and the commitment to support, also financially, charitable, missionary, and cultural initiatives promoted or supported by the Fraternity.

For further understanding of the "spirit" of the Fraternity, we recommend reading the *Letter to New Members* in the Appendix (p. 151).

5.2. *MEMORES DOMINI*

The very name of this Association summarizes its purpose and meaning; it unites those people in CL who have made a choice to dedicate themselves to God on a path marked by the virtue which the Church calls "virginity."

In 1988 it was recognized juridically as an Ecclesiastical Association by the Pontifical Council for the Laity (cf. Appendix, p. 159).

The life of its members (lay men and women who normally live in houses made up of either men or women, following a rule of group living and personal ascesis) is governed by the call to contemplation, understood as the constant memory of Christ, and of mission, especially in the workplace. The conception of virginity is based on St. Paul's call to "possess as though not possessing." It is not in order to give up something that one makes a sacrifice, but rather to possess reality completely – analogous to Christ's possession.

The *Memores Domini* are thus a potent call, to themselves, to the entire community and the workplaces where they operate, to the fact that the Lord creates and possesses reality and history and that everything is *made up* of Him. They are for themselves and others a sign that recalls what was revealed by the Christian event. In fact, it is only by the loving presence of Christ, by a complete dedication – of affection and intelligence – to Him that a boy or a girl can find it reasonable to obey a vocation that leads them to live everything not "less" but, like the character Pierre de Craon, the cathedral builder in Paul Claudel's *Annunciation to Mary*, on "a different level"[37] from others.

Besides, this call to the manner in which Christ possessed reality without possessing it is valid for the vocation to virginity as it is to the vocation to marriage.

The "Fraternity of Saint Joseph" is a new reality that has arisen from the Communion and Liberation experience. It is made up of those who wish to dedicate their lives definitively to Christ in virginity, while remaining in their current life situations.

Persons free of marriage bonds because widowed or unmarried – and this too is a vocation – have given rise to the first groups. These are men and women who wish to live a Christian life according to the Gospel tradition: in obedience, poverty, virginity, which are dimensions of faith, hope, and charity; faithful to the vows made at baptism.

Why become a part of *Memores Domini* or the Fraternity of Saint Joseph? And why marry? For the same reason that God gave at the beginning of the world: "It is not good for man to be alone. I will make a suitable partner for him:"[38] to live holiness as the supreme law driving everyday life, in a companionship guided towards destiny.

5.3. THE PRIESTLY FRATERNITY
OF THE MISSIONARIES
OF SAINT CHARLES BORROMEO

The Fraternity of the Missionaries of St. Charles Borromeo was born in September 1985 within Communion and Liberation as a priestly association. Encouraged by Father Giussani, the young priests who gave it life wished to support each other in their vocation and to respond ideally to the call expressed to the movement by John Paul II during the papal audience for the thirtieth anniversary of CL (29 September 1984) to go into all the world. The result was a missionary Fraternity, recognized in 1989 as a Society of Apostolic Life by Cardinal Ugo Poletti and as a Society of Apostolic Life by pontifical right on 19 March 1999.

Fraternity and mission are the governing words of this young community: to serve man in their availability to go wherever the needs of the Church and the life of the movement require the presence of priests, taking the experience of the movement into the whole world "by means of a priestly missionary energy," as its founder, Father Massimo Camisasca, has written. And to live a communion that is at the same time reciprocal aid and the method of a missionary presence in the various spheres: parish, school, university. The priests of the Fraternity live in "houses" that, disseminated by now over five continents, aim at being a sign to men of the companionship of Christ and an occasion for Him to be known from a new angle.

Milan Cathedral, 11 February 1998 – Holy Mass celebrated
by Cardinal Archbishop Carlo Maria Martini for
the members of the Fraternity of Communion and Liberation
of the Ambrosian Diocese on the occasion of the anniversary
of its pontifical recognition. Photo: A. Ascione

The Fraternity of St. Charles Borromeo thus lives a fundamental and continuing reference to the CL movement. It is made up of men who wish to belong to the movement and to let themselves learn constantly from its charism. The Fraternity especially wants, by its very existence, to demonstrate that the charism granted to Father Giussani is capable of educating and sustaining on the priestly path young men who have received or brought to fruition their vocation through the movement and who are called to live their priesthood for all the Church and for all their life.

5.4. CONGREGATION OF THE SISTERS OF CHARITY OF THE ASSUMPTION

Falling under the charism imparted to Msgr. Giussani is also the religious Institute of the Sisters of Charity of the Assumption, established in 1993 by Pontifical Decree as an autonomous Institute, separate from that of the Little Sisters of the Assumption, into which many young women from CL had entered from the Sixties onwards. Father Giussani had in fact been deeply impressed by the simplicity and charity with which these nuns lived and had recognized an accord with his own way of understanding and living the Christian life, so that he had directed toward this experience the vocations that arose within the movement which were most sensitive to the aspect of charity. Events within the Church after Vatican II led to a progressive differentiation, culminating in the birth of a new religious family, which finds in Msgr. Giussani the guide for living today the charism of its founder, Father Stephen Pernet, who lived in France in the nineteenth century.

Struck by the material and moral misery in which workers' families lived and their distance from the Church, Father Pernet gave rise to a work in which women who were living a total devotion to Christ in the religious life placed themselves at the families' service, sharing their concrete need through caring for the sick and helping in the home, witnessing in this way to the love of Christ present in the Church and reawakening faith by means of charity. This was from its beginnings an apostolic work, aimed, as its founder said, at "remaking a people for God."

The Sisters of Charity of the Assumption continue today the same mission, taking into account the changes in society that often make it necessary for them to work, without losing their own identity, within the network of services set up by local administrations. Their work is aimed at the family, through work in the home, caring for the sick, for children in difficulty, the elderly, always with full respect for the dignity of the person, who is worthy of respect for the sole fact that he or she exists. The result is a fascinating adventure in sharing, in which man is given value because he was wanted and loved by Christ, and his story has a meaning because it has a destiny of hope. The Fraternity of CL is the sphere in which the offer is made to the families who reawaken to the Christian call to pursue their journey toward a more mature life of faith.

The Institute is today made up of 81 nuns, 62 who have taken perpetual vows and 19 in the various stages of formation. The itinerary of their formation, faithful to the characteristics of the religious life in the Church, follows closely in method and contents that of *Memores Domini*, recognizing in it the unparalleled richness that Msgr. Giussani's charism offers for articulation of the experience of virginity. The Sisters are present in Italy with six communities, in the cities of Milan, Turin, Trieste, Rome, and Naples, and are preparing to found one in Colombia.

All these various forms of association are represented by rights in the Central Diaconia of the Fraternity of CL.

6

AN EXAMPLE OF ADULT, FREE,
AND RESPONSIBLE SOCIAL INITIATIVE

The Company of Works is a non-profit organization established on 11 July 1986, the result of the free initiative of young university graduates – CL members and otherwise – as a living witness to an education and a mature faith. The association's aim is to "promote the spirit of mutual collaboration and aid for an optimal utilization of resources and energies, to aid the insertion of young people and the unemployed into the world of work, continuing the social presence of Catholics and in light of the teachings of the magisterium of the Church" (from art. 4 of the Statute).

The Company of Works unites in a network about 10,000 members between small and medium-sized businesses, charitable and cultural associations, and non-profit organizations, with headquarters in Italy and abroad.

The Company represents a unique element in the panorama of civic associations: it is not a corporation or a holding company, nor an offshoot of political parties, nor involved in defending the interests of any category. It does not participate in the management of its members' organizations.

The "glue" holding the Association together is the shared recognition that a commitment undertaken with the ideals of mutuality, attention to need, and the development of talents improves the quality of work and of social and economic life.

In these years, the Company of Works has been the prime mover and arena for the cultural articulation of important civic battles fought under the banner "More society, less State": those for freedom of education and for recognition of the principle of subsidiarity. The guiding line of these initiatives can be found in the conviction that it is the task of the State to favor and not to repress the free initiative of the individuals and organizations making it up, and that failure to do so results in the impoverishment of society, the decay of the State itself, and a dangerous ideological uniformity.

APPENDIX

New York, United Nations Building, 11 December 1997 –
Presentation of the English edition of *The Religious Sense*
by Father Giussani, organized by the permanent observer
of the Holy See at the United Nations, Archbishop Renato
Martino. David Schindler, Shingen Takagi, and
David Horowitz took part. Photo: S. Ricci

HOW A MOVEMENT IS BORN*

How was the experience of the movement Communion and Liberation born? What factors brought it into being and what is its origin still today? We are interested in what the beginning was like for you personally.

To tell the truth, it is a bit awkward for me to answer your question, because an account of what went into the creation of and what continues to underlie an experience like ours has already been recounted and published (cf. *Communione e Liberazione*, interviews with Msgr. Giussani, edited by Robi Ronza. [Milan: Jaca Book, 1976]). But it is also true that one can always speak about what one loves: even when you repeat yourself, new things emerge from what you say – because a true heart is always new.

How is a movement born? How is a Christian experience born? From a testimony, through a gift of the Holy Spirit – but I'll speak in greater depth about this later on.

A daily newspaper with a large national circulation recently commemorated the figure of Andrea Emo, describing him as a great but neglected thinker. The

* Notes from a talk by Msgr. Giussani at the international meeting of Communion and Liberation leaders in August 1989, now in L. Giussani, *L'avvenimento cristiano* (Milan: BUR, 1993, 29–50).

paper published a number of excerpts from his writings, among which was the following: "The Church was for many centuries the protagonist of history; then it took on the no less glorious role of the antagonist of history. Today it is merely the courtesan of history." Here is the point: we do not want to live the Church as the "courtesan of history." If God came into the world, it is not to be a courtesan, but rather our redeemer and savior, the focus of our total affection, the truth of man. And this is the passion that torments us and determines our every move. We can make mistakes in the moment of a decision, obviously, but the only aim we strive for is this: that the Church should not be the courtesan, but the protagonist of history. This immanence of the Church in history starts from me, from you, wherever I am, wherever you are.

In one of the Pope's talks to young people in Scandinavia, there is a phrase which sums up the entire content of our message to ourselves and thus to others. We want to shout it to the world: "Like all the young people of the world, you are in search of what is important and central in life," the Pope said. "Even though some of you are very far away from a geographical standpoint and some may also be far from faith and trust in God, you have come here because you are truly seeking something important upon which to base your lives. You want to put down strong roots and you perceive that religious faith is an important part of the full life that you desire. Permit me to tell you that I understand your problems and your hopes. For this reason, young friends, I want to speak to you today about the peace and joy that may be found, not in possessing, but in being. And *being is affirmed through knowing a person and through living according to his teaching. This person is called Jesus Christ, our Lord and Friend. He is the center, the focal point, he who unites everything in love.*"

If I may, I would like to repeat: "We know nothing other than this!"

"AND THE WORD WAS MADE FLESH"

How did this truth appear on my horizon in a way that it suddenly and unexpectedly embraced my life? I was a young seminarian, in Milan, a good, obedient, exemplary boy. But, if I remember correctly what Concetto Marchesi says in his study of Latin literature, "art needs men who are moved, not men who are devout." Art, that is, life, if is to be creative, that is, if it is to be "alive" – needs men who are moved, not pious. And I had been a very devout seminarian, with the exception of an interval during which the poet Leopardi, for a month, gripped my attention more than Our Lord.

Camus says in his *Notebooks*: "It is not by means of scruples that man will become great; greatness comes through the grace of God, like a beautiful day." For me, everything happened like the surprise of a "beautiful day," when one of my secondary school teachers – I was then 15 years old – read and explained to us the prologue of the Gospel of St. John. At that time in the seminary, it was obligatory to read that prologue at the end of every Mass. I had therefore heard it thousands of times. But the "beautiful day" came: everything is grace.

As Adrienne von Speyr says, "Grace overwhelms us. That is its essence [grace is the Mystery which communicates itself; the essence of the Mystery's communication is that it overwhelms us, fills us]. It does not illuminate point by point, but irradiates like the sun. The man upon whom God lavishes Himself ought to be seized by vertigo in such a way that he sees only the light of God and no longer his own limits, his own weakness [for this reason, the attitude of those who are scandalized by the enthusiasm of a young person who has had the experience of the "beautiful day" is ignoble]. The person who sees only the light of God should renounce every equilibrium (sought by himself), he should give up the idea of a dialogue between himself and God as between two partners and become a simple receiver with arms spread wide yet unable to grasp, because the light runs through everything and remains untouchable, representing much more than our own effort could receive."

Forty years later, reading this passage from Von Speyr I understood what had happened to me then, when my teacher explained the first page of the Gospel of Saint John: "The Word of God, or rather that of which everything was made, was made flesh," he said. "And therefore Beauty was made flesh, Goodness was made flesh, Justice was made flesh, Love,

Life, Truth were made flesh. Being does not exist in a Platonic nowhere; it became flesh, it is one among us." And then I recalled a poem by Leopardi, a poem I had studied during that month of "escape" in my third year of high school, entitled: *To His Lady."* It was a hymn not to one of Leopardi's many "loves," but to the discovery that he had unexpectedly made, at that summit of his life from which he would later decline, that what he had been seeking in the lady he loved was "something" beyond her, that was made visible in her, that communicated itself through her, but was beyond her. This beautiful hymn to Woman ends with this passionate invocation: "If you, my love, are one / Of those undying forms the eternal mind / Will not transform to mortal flesh, to try funereal sorrows of ephemeral beings; / Or if you dwell in one / of those innumerable worlds far off / In the celestial swirl, / Lit by a sun more stunning than our own, / And if you breathe a kinder air than ours, / Then from this meager earth, / Where years are brief and dark, / This hymn your unknown lover sings, accept." And in that instant I thought how Leopardi's words seemed to be begging, 1,800 years later, for something that had already happened, announced by St. John the Baptist: "The Word was made flesh." Not only had Being (Beauty, Truth) not disdained to clothe its perfection in flesh, and to bear the toils of this human life but it had come to die for man. "He came to his own and his own received him not"; he knocked on the door of his own home and was not recognized.

That is the whole story. My life as a very young man was literally invaded by this; both as a memory that continually influenced my thought and as a stimulus to make me reevaluate the banality of everyday life. The present moment, from then on, was no longer banal for me. Everything that existed – and therefore everything that was beautiful, true, attractive, fascinating, even as a possibility – found in that message its reason for being, as the certainty of a presence and a motivating hope which caused one to embrace everything.

On my desk at that time I had a picture of Christ by the Italian painter Carracci. Beneath the picture I had written a phrase from Möhler, the famous precursor of ecumenism whose *Symbolica* and other writings I had read at school: "I think that I could no longer live if I no longer heard Him speak."[39] Now, when I make my examination of conscience, I am compelled to beg Christ's mercy, through the compassion of Mary, that he make me return to the simplicity and courage of that time, because when such a "beautiful day" happens and one unexpectedly sees something of extraordinary beauty, one cannot help but speak about it to one's friends. One cannot help but cry out: "Look there!" And that's what happened.

STUDIUM CHRISTI

It happened already in the seminary, with some of the students who sat near me in our large classes (we were very numerous). So a small group began to take form

– because the same law is always at work: *a few grow closer, feel an affinity* with your vision, with your heart, with your life. And so the first true core of the Movement, which we called *Studium Christi* at the time, was born. Each month – later every two weeks – we put together a kind of mimeographed sheet entitled *Christus*, in which each of us wrote about his personal experience of the relationship between Christ's presence and something that interested him: studies, current events, other things. But another group of fellow students made fun of our efforts; they began to hold meetings and took the name *Studium Diaboli*. Man is capable of anything in his freedom. Then, a year and a half later, the rector of the seminary, who later became the cardinal of Milan, asked to see me. "What you are doing is a wonderful thing," he said. "But it is dividing the class and you can't do it any more." When he later became bishop of Milan, he used to tell the story, exaggerating poetically as he was inclined to do, that one winter evening while we seminarians were entering the refectory *en masse* and he was walking behind us without our being aware that he was there, he heard me say to another seminarian: "The rector has killed our 'Christ'." To tell the truth, I do not recall having said it.

In any case, these are things one cannot stop. The seed which I have described animated our friendship throughout our years in the seminary. It determined our choice of authors to read and which authors became our favorites (reading, for example, in high school Möhler, Solov'ev, Newman, understanding what we could). In this way we made our study of theology come alive. It certainly did not remain fossilized doctrine for us.

"HE CAME UNTO HIS OWN AND HIS OWN RECEIVED HIM NOT"

After about a decade of various experiences, while I was teaching at the same theological seminary, I met a group of students on the train to Rimini. I began to talk about Christianity with them. I found them so unaware of the most elementary things, and so indifferent to them, that I felt an uncontrollable desire to share my experience with them. I wanted them to have, as I had had, the experience of the "beautiful day." After that meeting I left my position at the seminary, in agreement with the rector (I was, in fact, spending more time with young people than preparing my lectures), and began to teach religion in Italy's secondary schools.

I still remember perfectly the day, so important for my life, when I walked up the four steps to the school's entrance for the first time. I was saying to myself: "I am coming here to give to these young people what was given to me." I repeat this all the time, because that was the *only reason* we have done what we have done (and will continue to do it as long as God allows us to). The only reason for our every move is *that they should know Him*, that men should know

Christ. God became man, and came unto his own; that his own people should not know him is the worst sin, is the greatest injustice, beyond compare.

CHRIST – CENTER OF THE COSMOS
AND OF HISTORY

"Christ – center of the cosmos and of history." When I heard John Paul II in his first address use this phrase (literally the same phrase – and my friends of the time can bear witness to the fact – had been from the beginning the one we used regularly for meditation), I felt an emotion that brought back all the memories of the discussions I had held with young people at school and which they had held between themselves, and the profound tension with which we gathered together in the name of the Father, of the Son and of the Holy Spirit. I always used to say to the young people: "Come and see," or "You will see greater things than this," as Jesus says in the Gospels. Or, as the prayer during Mass says, "May your Church be made manifest to the world," or "God, Glory of His people." And then I would ask: "But what is the meaning of 'God, Glory of His people,' if not the change that Christ produces in the individual and in society through the mystery of His permanence in the Church?" *This change is the miracle which gives Him glory.*

This is what we have been asking of God for so many years, only this: that Christ help us to live the Church in such a way that, even through our lives, our action, our companionship, our projects, He may appear ever more in the world to the men and women chosen by the mystery of the Father, that the glory of God may thus appear ever more clearly, through our adherence to Christ that changes our lives, and the life of the world, by transfiguring them. This is the sole reason we came together and will continue to come together, for as long as God wills.

When I first began to teach religion, I would ask the students I passed on the steps – students I didn't know: "Do you think Christianity is present here at the school?" Almost all would look at me surprised and laugh, and some would say, "No way!" So I'd answer: "In that case, either faith in Christ isn't true, or a new way of believing is needed." This is how our discussions began, starting from the premise that Christ was the center of the cosmos and of history, the keystone of knowledge of man and the world, the source of a possible peace for the individual heart and for society, the source of an unknown and unique impetus of affection, like the emotion Socrates describes when he suddenly interrupts his talk and says (to Plato, Xenophon, and his other listeners): "Is it perhaps not true, my friends, that when we speak of truth we even forget about women?"

Young people slowly became attracted to the debates we were holding, showing their curiosity, anger and affection. These became the most talked about subject in the school during the 12 years I served there as a religion teacher. *Christ and the Church* was the daily topic and the subject of ferocious debate.

I used to ask the young people (and still ask the question now): "What alternative do we have? The *political* alternative? On this point, Camus again has something to say in his *Notebooks*, written in 1953. Speaking about the political left, which at that time was the redemptive honesty of political energy, Camus said: "What the left approves of is done without a word being said, or else it is judged inevitable. This includes: 1. The deportation of thousands of Greek children. 2. The physical destruction of the Russian peasant class. 3. The millions in concentration camps. 4. Imprisonment for political reasons. 5. Daily political executions. 6. Anti-Semitism. 7. Stupidity. 8. Cruelty. The list could go on." But this list is sufficient for me. I don't mean to be pessimistic, but it is difficult not to view contemporary politics within this framework.

Then I would ask the students: "Is there another area of hope, more serious than politics, more able to succeed? Is it *science*?" Thirty years ago, "science" was a word one hundred times more "divine" than it is today. We had to wait many years later to hear John Paul II say: "The science of totality (because it is not science if it does not claim to deal with the total horizon) leads spontaneously to the question of totality itself, a question that does not find its answer within such a totality." Passion for the whole horizon leads inevitably to the question about the meaning of the horizon, but within it no answer can be found.

The development of our interest in life in all of its aspects had, and continues to have, his presence as its reference point: "We believe in Christ who died and rose again, *Christ present here and now.*" This interest has led us to become involved in politics in its overall meaning, in perfect awareness that it is not from politics that our salvation comes; and this made us regain enthusiasm all over again for studies and science, not out of a kind of idolatry or in order to advance professionally, but for a seriousness that could dig a deeper and deeper furrow for knowledge, which ultimately has its center in Christ. Our experience of his presence generated a passion for social and political life and a passion for knowledge (our movement's "Meeting" in Rimini, Italy, even if only tentatively, but with determination and passion, was born from this dual interest, that is, from the root that created this dual interest).

St. Augustine in his *Contra Iulianum* wrote: "This is the horrible root of your error: you claim that the gift of Christ consists in his example, while that gift is his person itself." Everyone speaks reverently about Christ's example, about moral values, even those who write in the *Voce Repubblicana*; indeed, they teach and preach to Christians that they must follow moral values for the good of the State. But the gift of Christ is his presence; this is the new thing in the world and there will never be anything newer than this.

In one of his poems, Milosz writes: "I am only a man, therefore I need perceivable signs; constructing ladders of abstractions tires me quickly. Grant oh God, therefore, a man in any place whatsoever on earth and permit me to admire you by looking upon him." Christ is the answer to this supreme human prayer. Christ's incarnation meets the needs of man's nature. It corresponds in an unimaginable way to a sensible need, to the living and passionate need of a man.

"WE ARE ONE"

In his inaugural sermon, the new archbishop of Cologne, Cardinal Meisner, poses a question which I would like to turn to now: "The eternal word of the Father was made flesh. And now, in the Church, he can be heard and touched by all men." *But what is the Church made of? Of you, of me.* This was the sudden discovery I made that month of October when I began to teach religion.

If God has become man and is here and communicates himself to us, you and I consist of one and the same thing. Between you and me, strangers, the strangeness has been lifted, or as St. Paul called it, the enmity; we are now friends. In contrast, I would say to the students: "You have been together in the same classes for five years, sitting in desks next to one another. You have connived for years, but you are not really friends. You go on vacations together, you study together, you have fun together but you are not friends. You are temporary companions; there is nothing between you that is enduring. None of you feels interested *in the relationship with the other's destiny.*"

I said this to make the point that *Christ is present in us precisely in our unity*, that unity into which we are placed by the act by which he seizes us, the sacrament of baptism. By seizing us in baptism Christ *places us together as members of the same body (cf.* chapters 1 to 4 of the *Letter to the Ephesians)*. Christ is thus present here and now, in me, through me, and the first expression of the change which is a sign of his presence is that I recognize that I am united to you, and that *we are one and the same thing.*

Chapter 3 of the *Letter to the Galatians* contains another passage we always quote in our community: "For as many of you as were baptized into Christ have put on Christ. There is neither Jew nor Greek, there is neither slave nor free, there is neither male nor female; *for you all are one in Christ Jesus.*" Whatever utopia man may have created, he has never even dreamed of the unity which Christ has created in us. If we recognise him, he acts, and our life becomes more human.

Christ makes our life more human. Thus the other Gospel phrase with which I used to challenge the students when I entered the school – a phrase I used every hour I taught – was: "He who follows me will have eternal life and a hundred fold here below." " 'He who follows me will have eternal life,' may perhaps not interest you," I used to say, "but the second phrase cannot help interesting you: you will have a hundred fold here below.' According to this, you will live a hundred times better your love for your girl or boyfriend, your father and mother; you will have a hundred times more passion for study, love of work, enjoyment of nature."

The need expressed by Milosz in his poem is precisely this: to encounter someone – visible and touchable – following whom will make us experience the hundred fold: "Raise up therefore a man in some place on this earth and grant that by looking upon him I may admire You" – this is Christ for man.

But Christ is in you and in me, and that is a tremendous thing (*tremendum mysterium*); it is the source of our responsibility and of our humility, something we must inevitably confront because *we are the physical sign of his presence.*

There were 15 of us when I used to say that our community is the real sign – even if temporary, provisional, laughable but great – by which he becomes *the object of a present experience.* From that original group of 15, by my last year of teaching we had become a group of some 300. But the number doesn't matter. After 12 years there might only have been just three of us, or two (this is the meaning of marriage as a sacrament: marriage is, and ought to be, a sign for the community because one discovers in it a union not born of flesh and blood, but of Christ).

The community, infinitely dilated, is the Mystery through which I can truly say to Christ with fear and trembling and love: "You." My discovery of this came at a certain meeting held on the [Ligurian] sea coast, at the top of a tower, in Varigotti.

THE COMMUNITY IS THE PLACE OF MEMORY

Memory is the consciousness of a presence that has begun and lasts: memory is the consciousness of his presence.

The great Italian post-World War II writer Pavese used to say: "Memory is a passion repeated." We live a passion for Christ, a *repeated* passion, because unfortunately there can be no uninterrupted continuity in us.

Pavese also says: "The richness of a work [that is, of a generation or of our life as a generation] is always revealed by the quantity of the past it contains." But it must be a past that can be in the present more powerfully than as a memory, because memory fades, it is like worn out clothes. Memory has become the most important word of our community: *the community is the place where one lives memory.*

I would like to detail some aspects of this *reality of the community,* a word that indicates a companionship that is not born of the flesh or blood but from Christ, whose life is memory. As St. Catherine of Siena said: "Memory has been filled with blood." Our memory is filled with the blood of the cross and of the glory of the resurrection, because the cross of Christ cannot be conceived without the resurrection. Thus Claudel rightly said, peace, which is the heredity that Christ has left us as the sign of his active and working presence, "is made of equal parts of sorrow and joy."

THE DRAMA OF A BATTLE

Above all the life of our community has never sup-
pressed *the sense of the drama* of life; it has never forced
anyone to take any particular step. It has always been
a passionate proposal but one well aware of the effort
which must be made by those who have heard the call.

Certainly the truth bears witness to itself in its own
proclamation: Christ's message is so much in keeping
with what man longs for that the individual who
hears it cannot help being struck by it. The memory of
Christ is the memory of a past which becomes so present that it determines the present more than anything
else that is present. But immediately afterwards a resistance arises. I used to say to the young people in
class, "As I speak to you, you seem interested and
your faces say unequivocally, 'That's true, that's the
way it is.' But afterwards, something diabolical, original sin, fills you with 'buts,' with 'ifs,' 'perhaps,'
'however,' 'who knows,' that is, with skepticism, to
make you try to escape from the evidence that has
flashed before your eyes." When this resistance arises,
the drama of a struggle begins.

Every human relationship is filled with drama – no
real human relationship exists that is not. This fact
touches its deepest point in the relationship with
Christ. And the drama does not at all consist in an hys-
terical exasperation, but in saying "You" with an
awareness of the difference and of the journey that
must be made.

"First my will [where resistance is located above all] and then my intelligence," a Lithuanian dissident has written, "resisted for a long time, but in the end I surrendered, and I won [the winner is the one who achieves self-affirmation]. This was not a capitulation in the face of the adversary but a reconciliation with the Father [with the origin of oneself]. His possession of me is my liberation." (In *The Religious Sense*,[40] a book containing my notes from my first years at the school, I developed this idea of the identification between being possessed and being free).

After only a year from the movement's beginning, with the students in my secondary school classes, we printed an anthology of Dionysius the Areopagite, with the Greek text facing the Italian, that contained one of the most beautiful phrases I have ever read: "Who could ever speak of the love of the man who is possessed by Christ, overflowing with peace?" This is what I meant by the phrase, "His possession of me is my liberation."

ASKING: MAN'S SUPREME GESTURE

When I saw the human drama being lived by these young people – there were several hundred of us who would get together to discuss things from morning to night, even outside school hours – I understood for the first time, after all my years in seminary, what it meant *to ask*.

Asking is the supreme expression of man, and it is the most elementary one: man can ask no matter what condition he is in – even if he is atheist. Indeed, the more man feels in difficulty, the more the act of asking suits him. In Manzoni's novel *I Promessi Sposi*, the atheist – the Unnamed – says: "God, if you are there, reveal yourself to me." Nothing could be more rational than this: 'If you are there' *is the category of possibility,* an unrenounceable dimension of an authentic reason, 'reveal yourself to me' *is asking."*

We will all be judged according to whether we asked, because even in the lion's den or buried beneath the mire we can cry out, we can ask. During Holy Week, the Ambrosian liturgy suggests a moving form of this entreaty (the tenderness the Church can show is astonishing): "Even if I am late, do not close your door. I have come to knock. To one who seeks you weeping, open the door, merciful Lord; receive me in your dwelling, give me the bread of the Kingdom."

I never said to the first young people who met together: "Pray." All those who came, even if they didn't participate in its content, took part in the gesture of prayer. After a little while everyone began to take daily communion. I used to say to them that the *sacrament* is the greatest prayer, the essence of prayer, because *it expresses the entreaty of one's whole self:* one participates in it without even knowing how to think, how to speak, without knowing anything, asking by one's presence: "I am here." How can one, then, establish a hierarchy of values and contents? What must we obtain to be able to develop life? *What must one ask for?* Affection for Christ!

St. Thomas Aquinas says: "The life of man consists in the love that principally sustains him and in which he finds his greatest satisfaction" (in the Latin meaning of "satisfaction," which implies fulfillment, completeness). The most beautiful thing in the history of our movement is that first hundreds, and then thousands of young people have learned, and now live, the love for Christ that alone permits one to love one's friend, or a woman, or oneself.

But how do we get this capacity for loving Christ? First and foremost, by *asking for it*. The religious history of humanity, that is, the Bible, ends with this phrase: "Come, Lord Jesus." It is an "affectionate" phrase, overflowing with "attachment." Until a few years ago, it was the formula that we used regularly in our community. Now there is another which we focus on: *Veni Sancte Spiritus. Veni per Mariam.* It is the same, more developed and aware.

AN ALL-ENCOMPASSING AFFECTION

A love that sustains life, in which man finds his fulfillment, must have as its content, its object something that can *pertinere ad omnia* (interest all things). In this regard, a well-known phrase of Guardini's comes to mind: "In the experience of a great love *everything* that happens *becomes an event in its own ambit*." If a man and a woman love each other with a profound love, then the bloody events of Tienanmen Square, a song one hears, or the sun in front of one's eyes, everything that happens becomes an event in its own ambit.

The object of love must be capable of encompassing everything. For this reason Communion and Liberation (which was once called Student Youth) has never organized activities that were not unequivocally educational. The choice of the mountains for summer holidays, for example, is not a chance decision (we did not go to the seaside from the outset because it is too distracting). In the mountains, the healthy human surroundings and nature's imposing beauty combine every time to help renew the question of being, of order, of the goodness of reality – reality is the first provocation which awakens the religious sense in us. With the necessary discipline, which has always been rigorously preserved (discipline is like the bed of a brook or stream: in it the water runs purer, clearer, faster; discipline is necessary because everything is recognized to have a meaning), the vacations in the mountains are proposed to people's experience as a foretaste, even if fleeting, of the Christian promise of fulfillment, like a little anticipation of paradise, and every detail has to convey that promise and make that anticipation come true.

What our movement is usually criticized for is in fact the sign of our greatness: *that everything happens within the horizon of the presence of Christ, that is, of our companionship.* We are criticized for the fact that the experience of the love of Christ is all-encompassing; but everything that is divided and separated from his presence will be destroyed! Division is the beginning of destruction. This is why we have always hated the word censorship. I would say: "You cannot censor anything, not out of a psychoanalytic passion, but so that everything may be revealed, cleared up, explained and assisted."

GLADNESS IN THE DEPTHS OF SORROW

The sign of a life that goes forward in love for Christ, that is, that adheres to and participates in his companionship, is *gladness*. "I have told you these things so that my joy may be in you and your joy might be complete." Christ said this a few hours before he died.

Joy alone is the mother of sacrifice, because sacrifice is not reasonable if it is not attracted by the beauty of the truth. It is beauty – "the splendor of the truth" – which calls us to sacrifice. As the Bible says in the *Book of Sirach:* "A happy man is also at peace when he sits down to his meal; he savors what he eats."

This joy, this gladness lie even at the depth of the most acute sorrow, a sorrow which at a certain point cannot be avoided: sorrow at one's own evil. To belong to our company means beginning to feel that the greatest sorrow is that of one's own evil, of sin. No one can say: "I will never again commit a sin," because keeping God's law – that is, following Christ – is a miracle of Grace, not something we accomplish by ourselves. This is why the point at which the freedom of the Mystery and man's freedom meet and embrace is in asking.

THE GREATNESS OF THE INSTANT

Another discovery has become a normal part of our history: *the greatness of the instant*, the importance of the moment, contingent reality, in which an endless series of solicitations by which the Mystery calls us come together (thus our greatest friends are the inevitable circumstances in which we find ourselves: they are the objective sign of the Mystery that calls us). Again in the Ambrosian liturgy there is this lovely prayer: "Grant, oh God, that the Church of Christ may celebrate ineffable Mysteries in which our smallness as mortal creatures is rendered sublime in an eternal relationship and our existence in time begins to flourish as a life without end. Thus, following Your design of love, man passes from a mortal condition to a wondrous salvation."

THE WONDER OF AN ENCOUNTER

De Lubac, in *Paradoxes and New Paradoxes,* observes that "the conformist [one who adopts the prevailing mentality, that is, who does not adhere to His companionship] looks at even the things of the Spirit in their formal, exterior aspect. The obedient person instead takes even the things of the earth in their interior and sublime aspects." For this reason it is necessary to cultivate a human gift that is natural to a child and becomes something great when it exists in an adult: *wonder*. As someone wrote to me: "Nothing is communicated except what is received freely (as by a child). And it is kept only because one is astonished." We therefore need to increase our capacity for wonder: "if you are not like little children you will never enter."

In the second part of the first chapter of John's Gospel, there is an account of how John and Andrew set out to follow Jesus. Jesus turned around and said: "What are you looking for?" "Master, where are you staying?" "Come and see." And they went and remained with him the entire day. Let us try to imagine who those two men were who followed Jesus, quite scared, and the young man who walked ahead of them. Who knows with what wonder they looked at him and listened to him!

Another page of the Gospel strikes me in the same way. It describes the moment when Jesus passed through the crowds of people in Jericho. The head of the local mafia in Jericho, Zacchaeus, climbs a sycamore tree to see him, because he was a small man. Jesus passes nearby and looks up to where the man had climbed, and says: "Zacchaeus, come down quickly, for today I must stay at your house" (Luke 19: 5). Let's try to imagine what that man must have felt. It is as if Christ had said to him: "I respect you, Zacchaeus, climb down quickly, I am coming to your house." But that encounter would not be true – it would be as if it had not taken place 2,000 years ago – if it did not happen today. One cannot follow Christ if one does not perceive that he is true today! The *encounters* with persons who look at us and understand us as Jesus looked at and understood Zaccheus, and whom we can look at, are *the most important things* in our lives. "*Look* every day upon the faces of the saints and take comfort from their words," is the invitation of one of the first Christian documents, the *Didaché*.

THE COMPANY, PLACE OF BELONGING

The community, the company where the encounter with Christ takes place, *is the place to which our "I" belongs*, where it attains the ultimate way of perceiving and feeling things – grasping them intellectually, judging them. Here one can imagine, plan, decide, do. Our individual "I"s belong to this "body" which is what our company is, and find in it the ultimate criterion for facing all reality. Therefore *our point of view* does not go its own way, but rather *commits itself to a comparison and in doing so obeys* the community, the company. As Rilke said to his wife, speaking of that brief but exemplary belonging that is the relationship between a man and a woman, "When something remains obscure, it is the kind of thing that does not demand clarification, but submission." We experience great submission in our community life: submission to the Mystery of Christ who makes himself present among us and walks with us.

Something Péguy said captures the point well: "When the pupil does nothing but repeat, not the same resonance but a miserable copy of the thought of the master; when the pupil is nothing more than a pupil, even if he is the greatest of pupils, he will never create anything. A pupil does not begin to create until he himself introduces a new sound (that is, in the measure in which he is not a pupil). It is not that one should not have a master, but one must descend from the other by the natural ways of filiation, not by the scholastic ways of discipleship."

This is what our community needs in order for it to become the source of mission throughout the world: not discipleship, nor repetition, but *filiation*. The introduction of an echo and a new resonance is natural in a son who has his father's nature. He has the same nature, but he is something new. In fact, the son can do better than the father, and the father can watch happily as the son becomes greater than he. But what the son does is greater only in so far as it realizes more fully what the father has felt. For the living organic nature of our community, then, there is nothing more contradictory, on the one hand, than the affirmation of one's own opinion, of one's own measure, of one's own way of feeling, and on the other hand, repetitiveness. It is filiation that generates, the process by which the blood of the father passes into the heart of the son – and generates a different capacity of realization. Thus the great Mystery of his presence is multiplied and spread, so that all may see him, rendering glory to God.

POPE JOHN PAUL II ADDRESSES CL
ON ITS THIRTIETH ANNIVERSARY*

Dear brothers and friends!

I wish first of all to thank Msgr. Giussani for his introductory remarks, as well as all the others who took part in this introduction.

1. I express my vivid joy at this encounter with you, who have come to Rome to celebrate thirty years of your movement's life and to reflect together with the Pope on your history as persons living in the Church and who are called to collaborate in intense communion, to bring the Church to men, to spread her throughout the world.

Looking at your faces, so open, so happy on this festive occasion, I feel an intimate sense of joy and the desire to demonstrate to you my affection for your devotion to faith and to help you to become ever more mature adults in Christ, sharing in his redemptive love for mankind.

The photographic exhibition, which I had a chance to admire as I came into this room, the words (of witness, stories, songs) that I heard a few minutes ago have permitted me to live again with you from the inside this period of your life, which is part of the life of the Church in Italy, and by now not only in Italy, in

* John Paul II, *Per il trentennale di Comunione e Liberazione*, 29 September 1984, in *La traccia*, 1984, 1027–8.

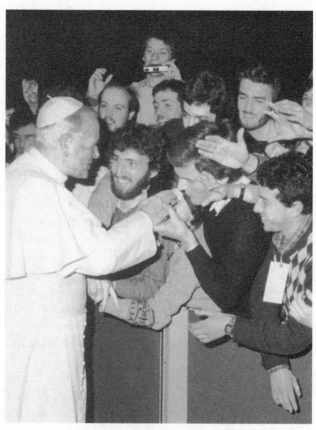
Pope John Paul II. Photo: Felici

our time. They gave me the chance to see clearly the educational criteria of your way of living in the Church, which involve a lively and intense work in the most varied social contexts.

For all this I am grateful to the Lord, who has once again shown me his mystery in you, which you carry and must always carry in the humble awareness that you are soft clay in his creative hands.

Continue in commitment on this path, so that through you the Church can be always and increasingly the place of the redeemed existence of man,[41] the fascinating place where every man finds the answer to the question of the meaning of his life: Christ, the center of the cosmos and of history.

2.   Jesus, the Christ in whom all is made and consists, is thus the interpretive principle of man and his history. To affirm humbly, but just as tenaciously, Christ as the principle and inspiring motive of your life and workings, of your conscience and actions, means to adhere to him, in order to make present in a sufficient manner his victory over the world.

To operate so that the contents of the faith become the intelligence and teaching of life is the daily task of every believer, which must be fulfilled in every situation and sphere in which one is called to live. And in this lies the richness of your participation in Church life: a method of education to faith so that it may affect man's life and history; to the sacraments, so that they may produce an encounter with the Lord and in him with your brothers; to prayer, so that it be invocation and praise of God; to authority, so that it be the custodian and guarantor of the authenticity of the path of the Church.

The Christian experience understood and lived in this way generates a presence that posits in every human circumstance the Church as the place where the coming of Christ, "a stumbling block to Jews and foolishness to Gentiles" (1 Cor. 1: 23–24), lives as the horizon full of truth for man.

3. We believe in Christ who died and rose again, in Christ present here and now, who alone can change and does change, by transforming them, man and the world.

Your presence, ever more consistent and meaningful in the life of the Church in Italy and the various nations where your experience is beginning to spread, is due to this certainty, that you must study more deeply and communicate, because it is this certainty which touches man. It is significant and noteworthy in this sense how the Holy Spirit, in order to continue with today's man the dialogue initiated by God in Christ and continuing throughout all of Christian history, has brought forth in the contemporary Church numerous ecclesiastical movements. They are a sign of the liberty of the forms in which the one Church is realized, and represent something new, which still awaits a full understanding of all its positive effectiveness for the kingdom of God at work in the today of history.

Some time ago my venerated predecessor, Pope Paul VI, addressing the members of the Florentine community of Communion and Liberation on 28 December 1977, declared: "We thank you for the courageous, strong, and steadfast witness that you are giving in this particularly agitated moment, disturbed by certain torments and misunderstandings that surround you. Be happy, be faithful, be strong, and be glad to bear witness all around you that the Christian faith is strong, is happy, is beautiful, and can truly transform in love and with love the society in which it finds itself."

4. Christ is the presence of God to man, Christ is the mercy of God toward sinners. The Church, the mystic body of Christ and the new people of God, brings into the world this tender loving kindness of the Lord, meeting and sustaining man in every situation, in every sphere, in every circumstance.

In this way, the Church contributes to generating that culture of life and love which is able to reconcile the person with himself and his destiny. Thus the Church becomes the sign of salvation for man, whose every longing for freedom she embraces and helps to develop. The experience of this mercy makes us able to accept those who are different from us, to create new relationships, to live the Church in all the richness and profundity of her mystery as the unlimited passion for dialogue with man wherever he is encountered.

"Go into all the world" (Matthew 28: 19), Christ said to his disciples. And I repeat to you: "Go into all the world to bring the truth, beauty, and peace, that are encountered in Christ the Redeemer." This invitation that Christ extended to all his followers and that Peter has the duty to renew unceasingly, has already woven your history. In these thirty years you have opened yourselves to the most diverse situations, sowing the seeds of the presence of your movement. I know that you have already put down roots in eighteen nations throughout the world: in Europe, in Africa, in the Americas, and I know also the insistence with which your presence is requested in other countries. Take onto yourselves this need of the Church: this is the task that I leave with you today.

5.   I know that you understand very well the inescapable importance of a true and full communion between the various components of the Church community. I am thus certain that you will not fail to commit yourselves with renewed ardor to the search for the best ways to carry out your activities in accord and collaboration with the bishops, parish priests, and all the other movements in the Church.

Take into all the world the simple, clear sign of the coming of the Church. Authentic evangelization understands and responds to the needs of the concrete man because it makes him encounter Christ in the Christian community. Today's man has a special need to have Christ before him, clearly and visibly, as the profound sign of his birth, life and death, of his suffering and rejoicing.

May the Virgin Mary, Mother of God and the Church, guide you constantly on the path of life. Knowing your devotion to her, I hope that she will be for all of you the "Morning Star," who illuminates and confirms your generous commitment of Christian witness in the world today.

And now with all my heart I give you my apostolic blessing.

Lourdes, 17 October 1992 – The pilgrimage to
commemorate the tenth anniversary of the Pontifical
recognition of the Fraternity of Communion
and Liberation. Photo: A. Ascione

Reverend Father Giussani,

After careful and extended study of your application presented to the Pontifical Council for the Laity on 7 April 1981, in my position as president of this Department, I have the pleasure today of sending you here enclosed the Decree of Pontifical Recognition of the "Fraternità di Comunione e Liberazione."

In fact, having reviewed the principles, aims, and organization of the Association as described in the Statutes you presented, where we see that the opportune amendments suggested have been adopted; taking into particular consideration the support manifested in numerous letters from Cardinals and Bishops; being aware of the spiritual and apostolic fertility demonstrated in the numerous and varied works that the Association promotes, supports, and creates; the Pontifical Council for the Laity has recognized that the "Fraternità di Comunione e Liberazione" fulfills the requirements for obtaining this recognition.

This approval clearly has as a consequence the commitment to ever greater loyalty, responsibility, and dedication to the Church. This Department thus considers it opportune to indicate to you the following pastoral recommendations which it does not doubt

[*] Vatican, February 11, 1982.

will be kept carefully in mind in the reflections and actions of the Association.

1. Of primary importance and pastoral urgency is the contribution that the Fraternity can bring to the Church by working together for the growth of a Christian, communal, and evangelizing sensibility and experience in the spheres – often secularized and "distant" – of the creation and dissemination of culture and the edification of society. A missionary presence in these spheres is seen to be more necessary than ever for bearing witness to Christ, as the Church, where the basic principles of human life and social interaction are at stake.

2. In times when it is felt that young people are searching in various ways for profound reasons and experiences that can give meaning to their personal and social life; in times when the Holy Father and the Bishops show a particular preference for the evangelization of youth, the Fraternity should intensify its commitment to being a propitious place of encounter and exchange of witness to the Christian life for the spiritual growth of the young people who approach it.

3. The consistent and enthusiastic affirmation of its "charism" and the profound "afectio societatis" resulting from it are undoubtedly fundamental premises for the creative and fertile development of every association. This affirmation is for the association a gift of

God. In this way the association puts down the deepest roots of its identity and originality. Experience has not shown in vain that the times of crisis and confusion of identity and goals of an association are manifested in the weakness and sterility of its projects and contributions. At the other extreme – in the case of a euphoric and uncontrolled exaltation of its identity and contribution – there is the risk of temptations arising within the organization toward an aggressive self-sufficiency. It is certainly important – and this must be the object of permanent revision guided by faith – to maintain a fertile balance between an associative "identity" and a meek "opening" to what the Spirit of God calls forth in human hearts, and especially in their multiform and diverse presence in the life of the Church. The fundamental horizon – which is certainly that of the Fraternity – must be of profound gratitude and meekness in face of the grace received through the Church and of total dedication to this gift for the good of all the Church as a sacrament of salvation for mankind. We know that we always "receive" much more than we "give." In this spirit of truth, communion, humility, the Fraternity will always be committed to making its "charism" bear fruit in the Church, with the Church, and for the Church.

4.   When the ecclesiastical nature of an association has been recognized, it is clear that it must live in complete availability and communion with the Bishops, headed by the Supreme Pastor of the Church. It is

particularly important, as the Statutes of the Association emphasize, that the Fraternity place itself at the service of the Bishop of each diocese and collaborate within the sphere of the pastoral work of the Church at a local level. In this context, I would like to recall the words of the bishop and martyr Ignatius of Antioch († c. 110), who in a letter to the community of Smyrna stated: "All of you must obey the Bishop as Jesus Christ obeyed the Father." There can be no doubt that here we have a fundamental theological principle of the Church. No spirit of division can arise from the Gospel. The Spirit of God is granted above all to those who come together to pray, as is often affirmed in the Acts of the Apostles with regard to the early Church. With its particular "charism" and teaching methods as a starting point, the Association will thus offer its experience and programs, integrating with and developing within the pastoral life of the diocese under the guidance of the Bishop. At the same time and in the same spirit it will participate in parish life, in a way that its presence in the "territorial" sphere of Church life and its presence in the different "functional" spheres be the stimulus to a balanced enrichment and complementarity.

5. The fundamental mission, also of the priests associated with the movement, is that of being "at the service of Unity." For this service they have been ordained and sent out by their Bishops for the care of

souls. They achieve this service every time that they fulfill their highest mission: that of presiding over the celebration of the Eucharist. They must therefore never neglect this service, nor take into consideration only the interests of their movement. Rather, they must be open to every charism that might manifest itself among believers, offering their complete availability and care.

6. It is true that the vitality of a movement depends also on the number of people making it up. And "Communion and Liberation," in the number of its members, represents a great strength for the Church. Precisely in situations like this, one must ensure that faith maintain all its strength of radiation onto life, and that seeking to fulfill the will of God and proclaiming his kingdom remain the Association's principal goal. It is true that effectiveness in society depends on the sizable number of its members; but it is also true that the spiritual effectiveness and the announcement of the Gospel depend on the spiritual activity and pursuit of a deeper faith on the part of the individual and of the group, through a life of prayer and encounter with Jesus Christ himself, through his Word, through the sacraments, especially those of penitence and the Eucharist.

7. When the Fraternity operates in various dioceses in a country and on a national level, it is of pri-

mary importance that its programs be worked out and its actions inserted into the framework of the pastoral orientations of the Bishops' Conferences, offering its collaboration and contribution whenever necessary and opportune.

8.   Communion and participation in the life of the Church demand a spiritual and practical openness to dialogue, collaboration and if need be to coordination with many other Church associations and movements, firm in the conviction that this is a mutually enriching exchange of gifts and a positive factor for the Church and its mission.

9.   The "Fraternità di Comunione e Liberazione," present mainly in Italy, nonetheless already counts local experiences in various countries. Its "catholic" and "missionary" vocation calls it to a progressive extension toward new secular and ecclesiastical realities. It will thus find a flexible way to adapt its identity and contribution to the very different expectations and challenges experienced in the manifold contexts of the Church in which it finds itself.

For its part, this Department remains particularly interested in maintaining periodic and regular contact with the Fraternity, for the exchange of experiences and programs of common interest, for the evaluation of the development of the Fraternity as an association and of possibilities of collaboration within the sphere of the participation of laypersons – and their movements and associations – in the life and mission of the Church.

Opilio Card. Rossi   Paul Josef Cordes
President   Vice-president

DECREE OF RECOGNITION

The "FRATERNITÀ DI COMUNIONE E LIBERAZIONE" originated in 1954, when the priest Father Luigi Giussani, with the aim of promoting communion as a fundamental necessity of life through a proposal of faith, began his apostolate of working with students, workers, and in general in the spheres particularly connected with collective life.

As a result of successive experiences, gradually brought to maturation and extended into different sectors of the associative life, the need was felt to educate to a more intense spiritual life, groups of responsible adults to whom could be entrusted the missionary apostolate in various fields of apostolic work, wherever the need was felt, who would place at the Bishops' disposal their energy and dynamic pastoral service.

As events rapidly evolved in most recent years and needs quickly changed also in the various sectors of the Church's apostolate, the idea also developed of a greater community collaboration, so that these adult groups came together in a lay association called the "FRATERNITÀ DI COMUNIONE E LIBERAZIONE," obtaining at the same time recognition as a juridical entity as described in canon 100 and canon 684, 685, and following the C.J.C., with a decree dated 11 July 1980, signed by the Abbot Ordinary of Montecassino Msgr. Martino Matronola, and under the auspices of the Patriarch St. Benedict, whose spirituality served as a guide to the above mentioned adult groups from the earliest period of their apostolic and missionary education.

The goal of the Association is to promote, as established in the Statutes, communion as a fundamental necessity of life, tending to express itself in a communal participation in the spirit of the Gospel, in ecclesiastical communion, keeping in mind that the dissemination of the Christian fact is generally conditioned by the presence of a community.

In particular the Association proposes, along with a more intense spiritual training for its members, proclamation and catechism at a capillary level, frequent celebration of the Sacraments, work in the fields of culture and the means of social communication, as an occasion for deepening and expressing their faith and as gratuitous service to others; and a commitment to missionary work as the meaning of the catholicity of the Church and as a vocational choice, in all the spheres mentioned in article 3 of the Statute.

Membership in the association can be requested by anyone who, as established by the Statutes, without distinction of sex or social condition, makes a written commitment to promote its goals, with a greater daily commitment to a life of communion as the most valid means of apostolate and a greater dedication to the service of the Fraternity, as compatible with the duties of each individual situation.

The members of the "FRATERNITÀ DI COMUNIONE E LIBERAZIONE" practice profitably their apostolate not only in many regions of Italy but also in other nations in Europe and on other continents, fostering exchange, communication, and dialogue and exercising a steady missionary presence in various sectors of cultural and charitable apostolate and social activity.

As the members of the "FRATERNITÀ DI COMUNIONE E LIBERAZIONE" wish to live their Statutes in a spirit of closer union with the Church and to participate more intimately in the mission of the Hierarchy in adherence to the doctrinal teaching of the Pontifical Magisterium and to collaborate in all the initiatives instituted by the Pontifical Council for the Laity, from which depend the associations of the faithful and the various ecclesiastical movements, the President of the Association, Rev. Luigi Giussani, has made application to this Department with the intention of obtaining pontifical recognition of the "FRATERNITÀ DI COMUNIONE E LIBERAZIONE."

The Pontifical Council for the Laity has not failed to examine, using the criteria of the Departments of the Roman Curia, the documentation transmitted to it, after having heard the vote of various consultants and experts and the opinion of qualified persons. Having received also testimonial letters from Very Eminent Cardinals, members of the Sacro Collegio and Residentials, from numerous bishops in Italy and other European nations and on other continents, urging pontifical recognition of the "FRATERNITÀ DI COMUNIONE E LIBERAZIONE," this Pontifical Council for the Laity, after having established that the Statute, corrected and revised according to the suggestions given, corresponds with the aims of the Institution, and having verified the clear and evident utility for the good of souls of the individual and community missionary apostolate that the members of the Fraternity propose to put into effect, ESTABLISHES AND CONFIRMS AS A JURIDICAL ENTITY FOR THE UNIVERSAL CHURCH THE LAY ASSOCIATION CALLED "FRATERNITÀ DI COMUNIONE E LIBERAZIONE," declaring it to all effects an Association under Pontifical Law and decreeing that it be recognized as such by all.

Any changes in the Statute that might be rendered necessary in the future by current canon law must be submitted for approval to the Pontifical Council for the Laity.

The Holy Father John Paul II, informed of the progress of the Association's application, in the audience granted to the below signed on 16 January 1982, was benevolently pleased to encourage the Pontifical Council for the Laity to proceed toward approval.

We thus express our vivid hope that under the protection of the Virgin Mary, Mother of the Church, and of the Patriarch Saint Benedict, Patron Saint of Europe and of the "FRATERNITÀ DI COMUNIONE E LIBERA-

ZIONE," the individual members and all the Fraternity together will give their clear witness to faith, as examples of piety and virtue that can always and everywhere act as the working ferment of an apostolate for the good of mankind.

Rome, 11 February 1982

Opilio Card. Rossi   Paul Josef Cordes
President   Vice-president

LETTER TO THE NEW MEMBERS
OF THE FRATERNITY

Following is the text of the letter from Msgr. Giussani which is sent to every new member of the Fraternity of Communion and Liberation.

Dear Friend,

I am happy to inform you that your request for membership in the Fraternity has been accepted. To help you be fully aware of the path that our company proposes to those who choose to belong to it, I offer for your reflection the text of my summary presented to the first Central Diaconia. If you feel uncomfortable with the seriousness of this commitment, please let me know.

1. *How the Fraternity of* CL *was born*

In the history of the movement of Communion and Liberation, the need has always been felt, by those who upon graduating from the university and getting married assumed adult status in society, to be able to continue a life of communion. After several attempts to respond to this need (for example Groups of Communion) and a certain period of perplexity (coinciding with the time after the student demonstrations were over), responding to the demand expressed by many recent graduates, an attempt was started toward the end of the 1970s whose name "Confraternity" gave the sense of its contents and image.

The historical phenomenon of confraternities was seen as the emblem of the needs we were feeling: the need, at first spontaneous and then the fruit of reflection, to live our faith and consequently to engage with it, together with the right to gather together freely and to carry out useful work in the Church and in society.

Subsequently, the Abbot of Montecassino, His Eminence Matronola, offering us the occasion to make a gesture on the XV centennial of the birth of St. Benedict, stimulated in us the idea of establishing a Lay Association that, under the auspices of the Abbey of Montecassino, would give a stable form to the attempts made up to then to form a Confraternity.

Thus a new movement began: the "Fraternity of Communion and Liberation," that increased and spread rapidly not only throughout Italy and other European nations, but also to other continents. On 11 February 1982, at the request of numerous bishops and with the encouragement of the Holy Father himself, the Pontifical Council for the Laity, who has the task of discerning the new charisms of movements and lay associations, granted the Fraternity its highest recognition, declaring it to all effects an Association under Canon Law.

2. *The "Fraternity of CL"* aspires to be an aware and committed, that is, mature, expression of the history of the CL movement.

It aims at being the level at which all the insights which by the grace of God have motivated and motivate us are realized, both in the sense of "becoming aware" of them, and in the sense of putting them into concrete form.

This does not mean that it is necessary, in order to belong to CL, to join the Fraternity, but rather that the Fraternity is an element of stability and completeness in the responsibility of the experience which is the life of the movement.

The aim of the "Fraternity of CL" is to ensure the future of the experience of the movement and its usefulness for the Church and for society. It does so through a continued emphasis on education and the realization of cultural, charitable and missionary works in the structures of society both in and outside the Church.

At this level I intend to take into consideration those persons who are willing to live it wholeheartedly.

3. *Adhering to the Fraternity* is a personal choice; it arises as a personal necessity for one's own faith and for the fulfillment of one's own Christian physiognomy. This is the only adequate reason to join.

In this sense, adhesion is totally free and responsible; the individual takes full initiative in this process. Thus unloading of one's own path onto a structure (as more naturally can happen with teenagers and university students) is eliminated as a factor.

To join the Fraternity, an application must be presented which, if accepted, allows one to enter the Association. It is in any case a personal choice and not one made by a group.

4. *The contents of this commitment*

a) To live the faith according to the spirit which the movement has always emphasized: faith is recognizing the event of a presence, God made present, who continues in history within the presence of a communion, of people who recognize themselves as gathered in his name.

b) Immanence, or being within, the Fraternity as a community of believers.

This means conceiving of oneself as inherent to this communion, in the totality of the factors making up life, and as self-awareness and self-image. The meaning of this companionship is that it is a vocational fact; it has an anthropological value, because one cannot conceive of a Christian if not within a companionship that is lived. Being inherent to this companionship involves adhesion to its organic structure (as established by the Statute) and obedience to its central directive body (the Central Diaconia). This availability to the company goes as far as the commitment of material aspects (money, time, energy ...) which are judged, according to one's personal conscience with regard to one's belonging to the Fraternity, to be functional toward achieving the common purpose.

5. An expressed communion of life is part of the *method of aid* to faith. This is seen as compared or analogous to monastic religious orders.

Expressed communion implies giving concrete form, as much as possible, to the unity which we recognize as ours.

The way this becomes explicit is thus the involvement of one's entire life, so that what happens to others cannot help affecting and engaging one's own life (at all levels, from spiritual to material). This involvement is real when it is freely entered upon by each one.

Communality of life is a principle by which to judge oneself and the things one does, more than being a quantity of things to be done. Thus there cannot be true communion unless it is filtered through each one's personal character and position in history. It must be visible that we are "one", the world has to see that Christians are "one". If we do not pursue this, with discretion and freedom of heart, and thus with joyousness of spirit, who can pursue it?

We must give the example of what it means to be one thing only, explicitly, expressly, according to the freedom and historical place of each person.

Instead, normally, involvement in a community is either relegated to certain forms or is asked for in a moralistic way.

Giving explicit form to communion of life means:

a) above all the search for a common path; therefore *spiritual aid* (gathering together for prayer, coming together for days of retreat or spiritual exercises ...);

b) the possibility of living together; therefore *social assistance*;

c) mutual *material help*.

This communal life is made explicit, verified and effected above all *at the level of the Fraternity as such* (like belonging to the totality of the Fraternity – to the company as it is guided and structured – otherwise group solidarity would eliminate the charity of the movement) even if there is on the regional or diocesan level a responsible person as an instrument of service to the groups making up the Fraternity movement.

Each group must have as essential characteristics:

a) a responsible leader, indicated by the group itself and recognized by the person responsible at the diocesan level (or, if there is none, then the person responsible at the regional level);

b) a rule of prayer;

c) a shared moment of encounter at periodic intervals;

d) a precise operative commitment which serves the common purpose.

Observations on work

Our work is established by our historic vocation: it is the movement. This commitment requires from everyone living the Fraternity an intelligent and generous willingness to work that takes the form, both at the personal and group level, of precise tasks and specific achievements in function of the work that is the movement.

In terms of method, this means converting one's own initiatives and activities and work experience into the reality of the movement.

As a corollary, the Center (Central Diaconia) could have an opinion concerning the necessity for a certain action in the context of the movement as a whole. Thus it is right that the members of the Fraternity, whether persons or groups, make all the sacrifices demanded to support this action before taking on others or giving this action priority over specific personal initiatives.

N.B.: From everything that has been said thus far, it should be clear that the origin of belonging to the Fraternity is the awareness of one's Christian faith awakened by the movement, a maturity in desiring its adult fulfillment and therefore the creation of a shared life that can be the instrument for achieving the movement's purpose and thus the purpose of the Church.

The result of this is the movement, whose expression is the multiplication of initiatives.

The path described thus leads from faith to works.

But the trajectory can also go in the opposite direction: some might gather together for a common initiative, and then, to give it consistency (that is, understanding that a more serious commitment to the faith is needed) they transform it into a Fraternity.

A person who wishes to participate in an initiative can be admitted to the Fraternity, as long as the personal choices and prospects for commitment are clear.

Common Fund

As witness to a communal concept of personal property, every member of the Fraternity participates directly in the Fraternity's common fund, pledging to contribute monthly a percentage (established by the individual) of his salary.

Whenever a group must support an initiative financially, the matter must be referred to the Central Diaconia. I ask you to consider this letter as strictly personal, and I pray our Lord that our shared path may be a good one.

Father Luigi Giussani

FROM THE STATUTE OF THE *MEMORES DOMINI* ASSOCIATION

The *Memores Domini* Association is a private universal ecclesiastical association, granted juridical status under Canon Law by decree of the Holy See.

The Association began in the Diocese of Milan as a *de facto* lay association in 1964, expanding the experience of the Communion and Liberation movement through the radical commitment demanded by the dedication of oneself to Christ in virginity.

After spreading into various dioceses, the Association was canonically recognized as a Pious Lay Association by the ordinary of Piacenza, Bishop Enrico Manfredini, on 14 June 1981.

The Association, established according to the norms of Canon Law (see Canons 298–311; 321–329) and according to its Statute approved by the Holy See, is composed of laypersons who commit themselves before God to living the Memory of Christ in their work.

There are thus two essential factors which may be discerned in the spiritual program of *Memores Domini*:

a) contemplation, understood as the continual remembrance of Christ. Christ is, in fact, the substance of all things (cf. Col. 1: 17), and he is present in history through the personality of the baptized and the communion of the brethren (cf. Gal. 3: 26–28), and

b) mission, that is, the passion for bearing the Christian message by means of one's own person transformed by the Memory of Christ.

The Association aims at effecting a missionary presence in order to bring the faith back into the lives of people, meeting them everywhere, in particular in their various places of work: in schools, offices, and factories.

The field of the apostolate, therefore, is essentially the working world. The Association recognizes that work is a normal condition in the life of every man. In the working world, a mentality which tends toward atheism and views work solely as an egotistic means of self-affirmation is often present. For this reason, carrying out the work of God ("This is the work of God, that you believe in the one he sent" [John 6: 29]) in the common condition of work constitutes the most acute aspect of Christian mission and the response to the signs of the times par excellence.

Each member of the Association commits himself to this mission by living his own job or profession as the place of the Memory of Christ, that is, translating every activity into an offering according to the teaching of the Second Vatican Council: "The baptized are consecrated to form a spiritual dwelling and a holy priesthood to offer spiritual sacrifices, by means of all the works of the Christian, and to make known the wonders of the One who called them out of darkness into his marvelous light" (*Lumen Gentium*, n. 10; cf. no. 34).

THE FULFILMENT OF A HISTORY

John Paul II's meeting
with the Ecclesial Movements
and the New Communities

Rome, St. Peter's Square, 30 May 1998

Rome, 30 May 1998[42]

> *"Suddenly a sound came from heaven like the rush of a mighty*
> *wind, and it filled all the house where they were sitting.*
> *And there appeared to them tongues as of fire, distributed*
> *and resting on each one of them. And they were all filled*
> *with the Holy Spirit."* (Acts 2: 2–3)

Dear Brothers and Sisters,

1.   With these words the Acts of the Apostles bring us into the heart of the Pentecost event; they show us the disciples, who, gathered with Mary in the Upper Room, receive the gift of the Spirit. Thus Jesus' promise is fulfilled and the time of the Church begins. From that time the wind of the Spirit would carry Christ's disciples to the very ends of the earth. It would take them even to martyrdom for their fearless witness to the Gospel.

It is as though what happened in Jerusalem 2,000 years ago were being repeated this evening in this square, the heart of the Christian world. Like the Apostles then, we too find ourselves gathered in a great upper room of Pentecost, longing for the outpouring of the Spirit. Here we would like to profess with the whole Church "it is the one Spirit … the one Lord … the one God who works everything in everyone" (1 Cor 12: 4–6). This is the atmosphere we wish to relive, imploring the gifts of the Holy Spirit for each of us and for the whole people of the baptised.

2.   I greet and thank Cardinal James Francis Stafford, President of the Pontifical Council for the Laity, for the words he has wished to address to me, also in your name, at the beginning of this meeting. With him I greet the Cardinals and Bishops present. I extend an especially grateful greeting to Chiara Lubich, Kiko Arguello, Jean Vanier and Msgr. Luigi Giussani for their moving testimonies. With them, I greet the founders and leaders of the new communities and movements represented here. Lastly, it is my dear wish to address each of you, brothers and sisters who belong to the individual ecclesial movements. You promptly and enthusiastically accepted the invitation I addressed to you on Pentecost 1996, and have carefully prepared yourselves, under the guidance of the Pontifical Council for the Laity, for this extraordinary meeting which launches us towards the Great Jubilee of the Year 2000.

Today's event is truly unprecedented: for the first time the movements and new ecclesial communities have all gathered together with the Pope. It is the great "common witness" I wished for the year which, in the Church's journey towards the Great Jubilee, is dedicated to the Holy Spirit. The Holy Spirit is here with us! It is he who is the soul of this marvellous event of ecclesial communion. Truly, "this is the day which the Lord has made; let us rejoice and be glad in it" (Ps 117: 24).

3.   In Jerusalem, almost 2,000 years ago, on the day of Pentecost, before a crowd astonished and scornful at the inexplicable change observed in the Apostles, Peter courageously proclaims: "Jesus of Nazareth, a man attested to you by God ... whom you nailed to the cross by the hands of lawless men and killed. But God raised him up" (Acts 2: 22–24). Peter's words express the Church's self-awareness, based on the certainty that Jesus Christ is alive, is working in the present and changes life.

The Holy Spirit, already at work in the creation of the world and in the Old Covenant, reveals himself in the Incarnation and the Paschal Mystery of the Son of God, and in a way "bursts out" at Pentecost to extend the mission of Christ the Lord in time and space. The Spirit thus makes the Church a stream of new life that flows through the history of mankind.

4.   With the Second Vatican Council, the Comforter recently gave the Church, which according to the Fathers is the place "where the Spirit flourishes" (Catechism of the Catholic Church, n. 749), a renewed Pentecost, evoking a new and unforeseen dynamism.

Whenever the Spirit intervenes, he leaves people astonished. He brings about events of amazing newness; he radically changes persons and history. This was the unforgettable experience of the Second Vatican Ecumenical Council during which, under the guidance of the same Spirit, the Church rediscovered the charismatic dimension as one of her constitutive elements. "It is not only through the sacraments and the ministrations of the Church that the Holy Spirit makes holy the people, leads them and enriches them with his virtues. Allotting his gifts according as he wills (cf. 1 Cor 12: 11), he also distributes special graces among the faithful of every rank ... He makes them fit and ready to undertake various tasks and offices for the renewal and building up of the Church" (*Lumen Gentium*, no: 12).

The institutional and charismatic aspects are coessential as it were to the Church's constitution. They contribute, although differently, to the life, renewal and sanctification of God's people. It is from this providential rediscovery of the Church's charismatic dimension that, before and after the Council, a remarkable pattern of growth has been established for ecclesial movements and new communities.

5.   Today the Church rejoices at the renewed confirmation of the prophet Joel's words which we have just heard: "I will pour out my Spirit upon all flesh" (Acts 2: 17). You, present here, are the tangible proof of this "outpouring" of the Spirit. Each movement is different from the others, but they are all united in the same communion and for the same mission. Some charisms given by the Spirit burst in like an impetuous wind, which seizes people and carries them to new ways of missionary commitment to the radical service of the Gospel, by ceaselessly proclaiming the truths of faith, accepting the living stream of tradition as a gift and instilling in each person an ardent desire for holiness.

Today, I would like to cry out to all of you gathered here in St Peter's Square and to all Christians: Open yourselves docilely to the gifts of the Spirit! Accept gratefully and obediently the charisms which the Spirit never ceases to bestow on us! Do not forget that every charism is given for the common good, that is, for the benefit of the whole Church.

6. By their nature, charisms are communicative and give rise to that "spiritual affinity between persons" (*Christifideles laici*, n. 24) and that friendship in Christ which is the origin of "movements". The passage from the original charism to the movement happens through the mysterious attraction that the founder holds for all those who become involved in his spiritual experience. In this way movements officially recognized by ecclesiastical authority offer themselves as forms of self-fulfilment and as reflections of the one Church.

Their birth and spread has brought to the Church's life an unexpected newness which is sometimes even disruptive. This has given rise to questions, uneasiness and tensions; at times it has led to presumptions and excesses on the one hand, and on the other, to numerous prejudices and reservations. It was a testing period for their fidelity, an important occasion for verifying the authenticity of their charisms.

Today a new stage is unfolding before you: that of ecclesial maturity. This does not mean that all problems have been solved. Rather, it is a challenge. A road to take. The Church expects from you "mature" fruits of communion and commitment.

7.   In our world, often dominated by a secularised culture which encourages and promotes models of life without God, the faith of many is sorely tested, and is frequently stifled and dies. Thus we see an urgent need for powerful proclamation and solid, in-depth Christian formation. There is so much need today for mature Christian personalities, conscious of their baptismal identity, of their vocation and mission in the Church and in the world! There is great need for living Christian communities. And here are the movements and the new ecclesial communities: they are the response, given by the Holy Spirit, to this critical challenge at the end of the millennium. You are this providential response.

True charisms cannot but tend towards the encounter with Christ in the sacraments. The ecclesial realities to which you belong have helped you to rediscover your baptismal vocation, to appreciate the gifts of the Spirit received at Confirmation, to entrust yourselves to God's forgiveness in the sacrament of Reconciliation and to recognize the Eucharist as the source and summit of the whole of Christian life. Thanks to this powerful sacramental ecclesial experience, wonderful Christian families have come into being which are open to life, true "domestic churches", and many vocations to the ministerial priesthood and the religious life have blossomed, as well as new forms of lay life inspired by the evangelical counsels. You have learned in the movements and new communities that faith is not abstract talk, nor vague religious sentiment, but new life in Christ instilled by the Holy Spirit.

8.   How is it possible to safeguard and guarantee a charism's authenticity? It is fundamental in this regard that every movement submit to the discernment of the competent ecclesiastical authority. For this reason no charism dispenses from reference and submission to the Pastors of the Church. The Council wrote in clear words: "Those who have charge over the Church should judge the genuineness and proper use of those gifts, through their office not indeed to extinguish the Spirit, but to test all things and hold fast to what is good (cf. 1 Thes 5: 12; 19–21) (*Lumen Gentium, n. 12*). This is the necessary guarantee that you are on the right road! [...]

In the confusion that reigns in the world today, it is so easy to err, to give in to illusions. May this element of trusting obedience to the Bishops, the successors of the Apostles, in communion with the successor of Peter never be lacking in the Christian formation provided by your movements! You know the criteria for the ecclesiality of lay associations found in the Apostolic Exhortation *Christifideles laici* (cf. n. 30). I ask you always to adhere to them with generosity and humility, bringing your experiences into the local Churches and parishes, while always remaining in communion with the Pastors and attentive to their direction.

9.   Jesus said: "I came to cast fire upon the earth; and how I wish that it were already kindled!"

(Lk 12: 39). As the Church prepares to cross the threshold of the third millennium, let us accept the Lord's invitation, so that his fire may spread in our hearts and in those of our brothers and sisters.

Today, from this upper room in St Peter's Square, a great prayer rises: *Come, Holy Spirit,* come and renew the face of the earth! Come with your seven gifts! Come, Spirit of Life, Spirit of Communion and Love! The Church and the world need you. Come, Holy Spirit, and make ever more fruitful the charisms you have bestowed on us. Give new strength and missionary zeal to these sons and daughters of yours who have gathered here. Open their hearts; renew their Christian commitment in the world. Make them courageous messengers of the Gospel, witnesses to the risen Jesus Christ, the Redeemer and Saviour of man. Strengthen their love and their fidelity to the Church.

Let us turn our eyes to Mary, Christ's first disciple, Spouse of the Holy Spirit and Mother of the Church, who was with the Apostles at the first Pentecost, so that she will help us to learn from her "*fiat*" docility to the voice of the Spirit.

Today, from this square, Christ says to each one of you: "Go into the whole world and preach the Gospel to the whole creation "(Mk 16: 15). He is counting on every one of you, and so is the Church. "See", the Lord promises, "I am with you every day to the end of the world" (Mt 28: 20). I am with you.

Amen!

"IN THE SIMPLICITY OF MY HEART
I HAVE GLADLY GIVEN YOU
EVERYTHING"

Msgr. Giussani's testimony during the meeting with the Pope, St Peter's Square, Rome, 30 May 1998

Your Holiness, I'll say, I'll try to say how an attitude was born in me – an attitude that God was to bless, as he wished – and that I could not have foreseen and not even wished for.

1. *"What is man that you should keep him in mind, mortal man that you care for him?"* (Ps 8). No question in life has ever struck me like this one. There has been only one Man in the world who could answer me, by asking another question, *"What would it profit a man if he gain the whole world, and then lose himself? Or what could a man give in exchange for himself?"* (Mt 16: 26; cf Mk 8: 36ff; Lk 9: 25f).

I was never asked a question that left me so short of breath as this question of Christ's!

No woman ever heard another voice speak of her son with such an original tenderness and unquestionable valuing of the fruit of her womb, with such a wholly positive affirmation of its destiny; it is only the voice of the Jew, Jesus of Nazareth. And more than that, no man can feel his own dignity and absolute value affirmed way beyond all his achievements. No one in the world has ever been able to speak like this!

Only Christ takes my humanity so completely to heart. This is the wonder expressed by Dionysius the

Areopagite (5th Century): *"Who could ever speak to us of the love that Christ has for man, overflowing with peace?"* I've been repeating these words to myself for more than fifty years!

This is why *"Redemptor Hominis"* came into our horizon like a beam of light in the thick darkness covering the earth of present-day man, with all his confused questions.

Thank you, Your Holiness.

It was a simplicity of heart that made me feel and recognise Christ as exceptional, with that certain promptness that marks the unassailable and indestructible evidence of factors and moments of reality, which, on entering the horizon of our person, pierce us to the heart.

So the acknowledgement of who Christ is in our lives invades the whole of our awareness of living: *"I am the Way, the Truth and the Life"* (Jn 14: 6)

"Domine Deus, in simplicitate cordis mei laetus obtuli universa" ("Lord God, in the simplicity of my heart I have gladly given You everything"), says a prayer of the Ambrosian Liturgy; what shows that this acknowledgement is true is the fact that life has an ultimate, tenacious capacity for gladness.

2. How can this gladness, which is the human glory of Christ, and which fills my heart and my voice in some moments, be found to be true and reasonable to present-day man?

Because that Man, the Jew, Jesus of Nazareth, died for us and is risen. That Risen Man is the Reality on which all the positivity of every man's existence depends.

Every earthly experience lived in the Spirit of Jesus, Risen from the dead, blossoms in Eternity. This blossoming will not take place only at the end of time; it has already begun at the dawn of Easter. Easter is the beginning of this journey to the eternal Truth of everything, a journey that is therefore already within man's history.

For Christ, as the Word of God made flesh, makes himself present as the Risen one in every period of time, throughout the whole of history, in order to reach the Easter morning at the end of this time, at the end of this world.

The Spirit of Jesus, that is to say of the Word made flesh, becomes an experience possible for ordinary man, in His power to redeem the whole existence of each person and human history, in the radical change that He produces in the one who encounters Him, and, like John and Andrew, follows Him.

Thus for me the grace of Jesus, in so far as I have been able to adhere to the encounter with Him and communicate Him to my brothers in God's Church, has become the experience of a faith that in the Holy Church, that is to say the Christian People, revealed itself as a call and a desire to feed a new Israel of God: "*Populum Tuum vidi, cum ingenti gaudio, Tibi offerre donare*" ("With great joy, I saw your People, acknowledging existence as an offering to You"), continues the liturgical prayer.

So it was that I saw a people forming, in the name of Christ. Everything in me became truly more religious, with my awareness striving to discover that God is all in all (1 Cor 15: 28). In this people gladness was becoming "ingenti gaudio", that is to say the decisive factor of one's own history as ultimate positivity and therefore as joy.

What could have seemed at most to be an individual experience was becoming a protagonist in history, and so an instrument of the mission of the one People of God.

This now is the foundation of the search for an expressed unity amongst us.

3. That precious text of the Ambrosian Liturgy concludes with these words: *"Domine Deus, custodi hanc voluntatem cordis eorum"* "Lord God, keep safe this attitude of their heart".

Infidelity always arises in our hearts even before the most beautiful and true things; the infidelity in which, before God's humanity and man's original simplicity, man can fall short, out of weakness and worldly preconception, like Judas and Peter. Even this personal experience of infidelity that always happens, revealing the imperfection of every human action, makes the memory of Christ more urgent.

The desperate cry of the Pastor Brand in Ibsen's play of the same name, ("Answer me, O God, in the hour in which death is swallowing me up: so the whole of man's will is not enough to achieve even a part of salvation?") is answered by the humble positivity of St Theresa of the Child Jesus who writes, *"When I am charitable it is only Jesus who is acting in me"*.

All this means that man's freedom, which the Mystery always involves, has *prayer* as its supreme, unassailable expressive form. This is why freedom, according to the whole of its true nature, posits itself as an entreaty to adhere to Being, and therefore to Christ. Even in man's incapacity, in man's great weakness, affection for Christ is destined to last.

In this sense Christ, Light and Strength for every one of his followers, is the adequate reflection of that word with which the Mystery appears in its ultimate relationship with the creature, as *mercy*: *Dives in Misericordia*. The mystery of mercy shatters any image of complacency or despair; even the feeling of forgiveness lies within this mystery of Christ.

This is the ultimate embrace of the Mystery, against which man – even the most distant, the most perverse or the most obscured, the most in the dark, – cannot oppose anything, can make no objection. He can abandon it, but in so doing he abandons himself and his own good. The Mystery as mercy remains the last word even on all the awful possibilities of history.

For this reason existence expresses itself, as ultimate ideal, in begging. The real protagonist of history is the beggar: Christ who begs for man's heart, and man's heart that begs for Christ.

Milan, 3rd June 1998

Thank you my friends!

What happened last Saturday, 30 May, happened because you, you too, are there, *together*. It is only togetherness that operates. Indeed, God is where unity is.

For me the encounter on Saturday with John Paul II was the greatest day of our history, made possible by the Pope's recognition. It was the "cry" that God gave us as a testimony to unity, to the unity of the whole Church. At least, that was the way I felt it: we are one. I said so, too, to Chiara and Kiko who were there beside me in St Peter's Square: how is it possible not to cry out our unity on such occasions?

And then I perceived – more intensely than ever before – the fact that we are *for* the Church, we are a factor that builds the Church. I felt myself taken into God's hands, Christ's hands, those hands that mould history.

These are times in which I have begun truly to understand – and all the more on Saturday – the responsibility to which God has called me. I had not understood, but on Saturday it was clear. And this responsibility is such in so far as it communicates itself to others precisely as responsibility. This is true when it is for the whole Church, and therefore for the whole movement; when it is an obedience to the fact that – as St. Paul says – "none of us lives for himself, and none of us dies for himself, since if we live, it is for the Lord that we live, and if we die, it is for the Lord that we die. Whether we live or die, then, we belong to the Lord." (Rom. 14: 7–8).

It is God who is at work in what we do: "God is all in all". Our responsibility is for unity, to the point of valuing even the smallest good that is in the other.

Affectionately yours,

Fr. Luigi Giussani

NOTES

1 F. Kafka, *Il silenzio delle sirene. Scritti e drammenti postumi (1917–1924)* (Milan: Feltrinelli, 1994), p. 91.

2 Cf. Tacitus, *Germania,* IX, 2.

3 L. Giussani, *At the Origin of the Christian Claim* (Montreal: McGill-Queen's University Press, 1998), p. 32–3.

4 V. Hugo, "Le Pont," in *Les contemplations* (Paris: Michel Lévy Frères-Hetzel-Pagnerre, 1857).

5 Cf. John 14: 6.

6 Rev. 3: 20.

7 Cf. Giussani, *At the Origin of the Christian Claim*, pp. 80, 98.

8 Cf. Mark 8: 33.

9 The images and text of this video were published in *30DAYS*, no. 2 (February 1995): 33–48.

10 John Paul II, "Ai movimenti ecclesiali," 2 March 1987, in *La traccia*, 1987, p. 190.

11 Cf. John Paul II, "Per il trentennale di Comunione e Liberazione," *La traccia* (29 September 1984): 1027–8.

12 *Ibid.*, 1028.

13 "Luigi Giussani, Fondatore di Comunione e Liberazione," in P.J. Cordes, *Segni di speranza* (Milan, San Paolo: 1998), 98–101.

14 T.S. Eliot, *Choruses from 'The Rock,'* in *Collected Poems 1909–1962* (San Diego, New York, London: Harcourt Brace Jovanovich, 1963), 163.

15 John 21: 15 ff.

16 This title would be used many years later (cf. 5.1) to identify the gathering together of groups of priests within the framework of the Fraternity of Communion and Liberation.

17 L. Giussani, "Il valore di alcune parole che segnano il cammino cristiano," in *L'Osservatore Rômano*, 6 April 1966, 4.

18 T.S. Eliot, *Collected Poems 1909–1962*, 164.

19 Matthew 19: 29.

20 Now collected in L. Giussani, *Il cammino al vero è un'esperienza* (Turin: SEI, 1995).

21 L. Giussani, "Come nasce un movimento," now in *L'avvenimento cristiano* (Milan: BUR, 1993), 35. Cf. Appendix, 00–00.

22 Federazione Universitari Cattolici Italiani [Federation of Italian Catholic University Students], an organ of Azione Cattolica in the university sector.

23 Cf. L. Giussani, *Il movimento di Comunione e Liberazione. Conversazioni con Robi Ronza* (Milan: Jaca Book, 1987), 54, note 4.

24 *Ibid.*, 56.

25 Associazione Cattolica Lavoratori Italiani [Italian Catholic Workers Association].

26 Paul VI, *Omelia per la solennità dei santi Pietro e Paolo*, 29 June 1972. Some years later, Paul VI would use even more dramatic tones: "what strikes me, when I consider the Catholic world, is that within Catholicism a non-Catholic type of thinking sometimes seems to predominate, and it could happen that this non-Catholic thinking within Catholicism tomorrow becomes even stronger … It

is necessary that a small flock continue to exist" (J. Guitton, *Paolo VI segreto* [Milan: Ed. Paoline, 1987], 152–3).

27 L. Giussani, "Dall'utopia alla presenza," in *Un avvenimento di vita, cioè una storia* (Rome: EDIT, 1993), 131.

28 John Paul II, *Redemptor hominis*, Encyclical letter, 4 March 1979, 1.

29 L. Giussani, "Natale, tempo di speranza per l'uomo moderno che non crede più in niente," in *Il Giornale*, 24 December 1996, 1.

30 J. Guitton, *Arte nuova di pensare* (Milan: Edizioni Paoline, 1986), 71.

31 E. Toaff-A. Elkann, *Essere ebreo* (Milan: Bompiani, 1994) 40.

32 L. Giussani, "Introduzione," in *Il rischio educativo* (Turin, SEI, 1995), xvii.

33 N. Lobkowicz, "Prefazione," in L. Giussani, *Il rischio educativo*, x.

34 L. Giussani, "Appunti di metodo cristiano," now in *Il cammino al vero è un'esperienza*, 115.

35 John Paul II, "Al Congresso del movimento ecclesiale di impegno culturale," 16 January 1982, in *La traccia*, 1982, 55.

36 1 Thessalonians 5: 21.

37 P. Claudel, *L'Annunzio a Maria* (Milan: Vita e Pensiero, 1990), 31.

38 Genesis 2: 18.

39 Cf. A.J. Möhler, *Dell'unità della Chiesa* (Milan: Tipografia e Libreria Pirotta e C., 1850), 52.

40 L. Giussani, *The Religious Sense* (McGill-Queen's University Press, 1997).

41 Cf. John Paul II, *Omelia a Lugano*, 12 June 1984, in
    La traccia, 1984, 656–9.
42 Osservatore Romano – weekly English edition, no. 22
    (1544) 3 June 1998, 2.

BIBLIOGRAPHY OF SELECTED WORKS

For a full listing of Msgr. Giussani's writings appearing in books or magazines, many of which have been translated in various countries, the reader is referred to the most up-to-date bibliography, published as an appendix to the volume *Porta la speranza. Primi scritti*.

Here we indicate the basic texts of Msgr. Giussani's works, and among them those with particular importance for the history and life of the movement founded by him.

Above all, the *PerCorso*, a series of three volumes entitled respectively:

- *Il senso religioso*, 1986, 1977[2]
  (English translation: *The Religious Sense*, McGill-Queen's University Press, 1997)
- *All'origine della pretesa cristiana*, 1988
  (English translation: *At the Origin of the Christian Claim*, McGill-Queen's University Press, 1998)
- *Perché la Chiesa*. Tome 1: *La pretesa permane*, 1990
  Tome 2: *Il segno efficace del divino nella storia*, 1992

The educational and catechistic itinerary set out by these texts serves as the basis for the work of the "School of Community."

These texts were published in Italy by Jaca Book and are currently being reissued by Rizzoli.

Other significant texts (we indicate the most recent editions, some of which are a collection into a single volume, at the author's behest, of writings previously published in various periods):

- *L'Alleanza*, Jaca Book 1979
- *L'avvenimento cristiano*, Bur 1993
- *Il senso di Dio e l'uomo moderno*, Bur 1994
- *Si può vivere così?*, Bur 1994
- *Il rischio educativo*, Sei 1995
- *Il cammino al vero è un'esperienza*, Sei 1995
  (this volume gathers the first three texts outlining the program of CL, published under ecclesiastical *imprimatur* between 1959 and 1964)
- *Il tempo e il tempio. Dio e l'uomo*, Bur 1995
- *Alla ricerca del volto umano*, Rizzoli 1995
- *Si può (veramente?!) vivere così?*, Bur 1996
- *« Tu » (o dell'amicizia)*, Bur 1997
- *Porta la speranza. Primi scritti*, Marietti 1997
  Among other works by Father Giussani:
- *Grandi linee della teologia protestante americana*,
  Jaca Book 1989
- *Pregare* (for children), Jaca Book 1984
- *Dalla liturgia vissuta: una testimonianza*, Jaca Book 1991
- *Un avvenimento di vita, cioè una storia*, Edit 1993
- *È, se opera*, supplement to « 30Giorni », 1994
  (English translation, *He Is if He Changes*, 1994)
- *Sulle tracce di Cristo.*
  Viaggio in Terrasanta con Luigi Giussani, Bur, 1994
- *Realtà e giovinezza. La sfida*, Sei 1995
- *Le mie letture*, Bur 1996
- *Lettere di fede e di amicizia ad Angelo Majo*, San Paolo 1997
- *Riconoscere una Presenza*, San Paolo 1997

Since 1994 Msgr. Giussani has directed a series published by Rizzoli entitled "*I libri dello spirito cristiano*." These are works of narrative, essays, and poetry, some of them hard to find because of cultural ostracism, and which document how a Christian spirit faces the problems of existence and culture. Among the more than thirty titles published to date are works (or anthologies) of classical Greek and Latin authors, G. Leopardi, T.S. Eliot, Ch. Péguy, E. Mounier, C. Dawson, J.H. Newman, A. Negri, S. Undset, H. Daniel-Rops, A. Gatti, V. Messori.

Spirto gentil is the title of a series of compact discs of classical music, from Pergolesi to Schubert, from Beethoven to Mozart and Russian choral music, issued by Deutsche Grammophon, which started in 1997 under the direction and with introductory notes by Msgr. Giussani.

For further knowledge of the history and identity of CL, at least up to 1986, the reader is referred to a book of conversations with Msgr. Giussani, edited by Robi Ronza, entitled *Il movimento di Comunione e Liberazione*, Jaca Book 1987.

Foreign publishers of all or some of the *PerCorso* texts, and of other works by Msgr. Giussani, are:

McGill-Queen's University Press (English); Ediciones Encuentro and Sudamericana (Spanish); Fayard and Le Cerf (French); Editora Companhia Ilimitada, Latinoamericana e Edições Paulinas (Portuguese); Johannes Verlag (German); Russia Cristiana (Russian); Wydawnictwo Michalineum (Polish); Zvon (Bohemian); F.D. Melissa (Greek); Vigilia Kiadó (Hungarian); Zdruzenie Jas, Lúc (Slovakian).

CONTACTING COMMUNION AND LIBERATION

Communion and Liberation is present in some 70 countries throughout the world. It can be reached most easily at:

General headquarters
Via Porpora 127 – 20131 Milan, Italy
tel. +39 02 26149301
fax: +39 02 26149340
e-mail: cl@comunioneliberazione.org
website: http://www.comunioneliberazione.org

International center
Via Calabria 56 – 00187 Rome, Italy
tel. +39 06 42011013
fax: +39 06 42011014
e-mail: centroint@comunioneliberazione.org

Litterae communionis – Tracce magazine
Via Porpora 127 – 20131 Milan, Italy
tel. +39 02 26149345
fax: +39 02 26149347
e-mail: cltracce@comunioneliberazione.org
website: http://www.comunioneliberazione.org/tracce

Traduzione dall'italiano: Susan Scott
Revisione: Amanda Murphy